# Blue Wizard Is About To Die!

## Prose, Poems, and Emoto-Versatronic Expressionist Pieces About Video Games, 1980-2003

### Seth "Fingers" Flynn Barkan
### Illustrated by Warren Wucinich

I'M AT ED

CELL #:

702.682.2951

CALL IF YOU WANT
INTERVIEW

### Rusty Immelman Press
### (R.I.P.)

For information, address Rusty Immelman Press, 4075 S. Durango Drive, Suite #111-72, Las Vegas NV 89147
www.twhi.org/immelman.htm
Immelman@twhi.org

Cover illustration: Warren Wucinich


ISBN: 0-9741000-0-5

# Contents:

## *Intro Cinema:*

This book of poems is the result of a lifetime's worth of research into the seedy realm of the video arcade ala les tres chic catastrophe known as the Eighties, a decade of shame and horror, excess, expense accounts, and credits... twenty five cents, the world seemed to bark, twenty five cents and, Yes, You Too (my diminutive eight year old friend) can BECOME the robotic holographic ninja... dare to dream, kiddo; dare to dream.

Having been born in Vegas (a unique tragedy in of itself) during the first year of that bleak decade, I grew up in these hives of digital activity, playing some of the greatest machines ever made. A few of these games are featured in this book; Sinistar, Dragon's Lair, Joust, Super Mario, and several others. Unfortunately, due to draconian limits placed on the number of pages that I'm allowed to print (imposed upon me by my alternate personalities, one of whom happens to be an accountant and former Nazi), I've been forced to leave a great many of the classics (and moderns) to wallow in their undeserved obscurity. There is not enough space for me to write all that I remember of the glory days of da sweaty fingered roll of quarters, sweet as eating a box of brown sugar, the gritty black dirt running in rivers, manically inserted with junky-DT-fingers into the slot.

That having been said, there are also poems in this book about games that did not appear in the arcades; some of them from consoles (home systems like the Nintendo, Jaguar, Colecovision, and Playstation 2), as well as others from the utterly awesome realm of computer gaming. No matter what, my premise while writing this book was to portray these games as being something other than the insipid and pointless rot-your-brain-ruin-your-eyes-waste-your-life-away-whydontcha entertainments that many of the adults of my youth saw them as, but as the works of art that they truly are. The golden era of video gaming and the arcades that once housed these mighty machines is drawing to a close, but the roaring twenties of this bold experimental art form is on its way. It is my prediction that, over the coming fifteen years, these games will be looked upon as the works of art that they truly are; I know this from the nostalgic pangs of regret, the vividness of memory, and the simple delight that springs to mind when I look through my catalogue of old cartridges and eviscerated hardware.

Speaking of which, no matter what revolutionary advancement in the hardware, and no matter how spectacular the graphics may become, the age of the utterly bizarre video-game as gameplay devoid of spectacle is lost forever. I try to bear tribute to these, the greatest games ever made, while also acknowledging their progenies' accomplishments at entertaining and delighting us.

One premise found within many of the works in this book deserves a little explanation and preemptive defense. Video games as providing a unique experience will probably offend most squares at first, but, when one stops to think about it, it's easy to see this "experience" as being an exact facsimile of the similarly useless indulgence of enjoying great works of art, be they a Tchaikovsky symphony, a jazz quartet, a movie, a book, a poem, a beautiful painting, or a stunning photograph. Just as the viewing/listening/ reading of these works provides and creates an experience to which we cling for the rest of our days, so do video games; we just haven't had time to realize this power exists within the medium.

I would also be remiss if I did not point out the title of this book, which contains a necessary declaration of poetic license run amok: this book is meant to appeal most to the people who played the games in question, recalling for them visceral memories of combat, blood, guts, screams of the dying, and all that other fun jazz. Likewise, a fair effort has been made to introduce the non-gaming public to the joys of pursuing such activities. Thus, several of these poems take on a more essayistic style, describing a clear narrative rather than trying to re-synthesize what is already a synthetic experience. This is poetry for the people, just as games are art for the people. I sincerely hope you enjoy my work, and encourage you to support your local arcade if you are fortunate enough to still have one.

Sincerely,
Seth "Fingers" Flynn Barkan
Las Vegas, August 28th, 2003

One more thing: After having read many poems in front of people, I've discovered that (very often) the pieces that are supposed to be funny get no laughs while the "serious" ones do. Gentle reader, please do not be confused; these poems (for the most part) should make you laugh; even the sad and serious ones have plenty of room for laughter. As far as I'm concerned, if I can make one person wet themselves in a public place, then my job as a poet is done. Thank you.

# Blue Wizard Is About To Die!

Prose, Poems, and Emoto-Versatronic Expressionist Pieces About Video Games (1980-2003)

"The time has come when scientific truth must cease to be the property of the few - when it must be woven into the common life of the world." -Louis Agassiz

"The [first] game I developed was a two-person space war game. There were two versions: one with gravity, one without. The one without gravity was more fun... This project resulted in U.S. Patent 4,179,124 ELECTRONIC VIDEO GAME. " -Jed Margolin

**DEDICATION (Hall of Champions):**
This collection is for:

Joe and Jake, two guys who I've enjoyed killing again and again.

My Mother, for reading ZORK to me and typing my responses long before I had gained these essential life skills.

My Father, for taking me to arcades and being liberal with the quarters.

The programmers, whose great work has gone unrecognized by the mainstream for far too long.

And, of course, for Sulla and "the boys upstairs" at C.Z.

# MARIO:

King Of Plumbers; cartoon hands
white gloves, a psychotic
jumping thing made of big
slabs of solid color punctuated
by black lines, giving him features;
old hand... old hand... the savior
of the princess, hero of the mushroom kingdom,
commander of the psychotic and useless power of Yoshi,
a creature so dumb and pointless that,
only you, my little mustachioed Italian freak,
would dare punch it in the back of the head,
as if to say
"ready the tongue!
          prepare to fire!"
mounted like a monkey on a dog at a rodeo;
you bastard, sent him - after jumping - to his death,
using his doomed back for leverage.

Jump those pits, flee into the safety
of the green pipes, spit those shells,
send up the flag at every castle in the kingdom,
for, I, the liberator, the conquering Italian hero,
have returned, again and again and again;
we're going to make millions doing this!
you and me, kid, millions.

# THINGS I'VE LEARNED:

that heroes do not die hard
they die just as stupid and dumb
as bears walking into a shotgun blast,
clumsy and unknowing, they trip
trip wires, pick up grenades
but can't find the pin;
they die falling, spinning horribly
into the abyss during an acrobatic display
of the ninjitsu arts,
they die at the hands of The Evil One
direct; one to one, and they still get slaughtered.

there is no such thing as a hero's death
so long as there is no CONTINUE?
screen in real life.
There is just the lonesome shuffling,
the slow mourn of the broken;
poor in spirit, with empty pockets,
wandering like Jews in a garden,
asking questions of every cabinet,
searching for answers,
shouting up at God: why did you betray us?

# THINGS I'VE EXPERIENCED:


you ever sneak up behind someone with a garrote and land
that fateful killing strike, steal his clothes,
and then head into the heart of darkness, the enemy installation?

you ever crack open a single bullet that you
hid in your gut, swallowed, when the guerillas
caught you, CIA boy?; you ever harvest that
gunpowder into an explosive bolt of freedom
blowing out the cell door, loping into the
sweet jungle danger night?

you ever liberate a town from the grips
of a biker gang? Eh?

you ever fight Revolver Ocelot, his patter
getting to you, searching through the columned
shadows of the storage room, looking
for his long white ponytail and TB cough?
"I love the smell of cordite; you know,
that sulfur smell?"

even better, you ever stand at the end of the universe
and dip your toe in its oblique waters,
feeling the time sickness suck at your bones
like leeches that must feed on the marrow of living memory?
you ever fight a samurai on a Russian steppe in
the year 2095 AD?
how about running a fiefdom? Where is Oda now, you
weak kneed fuck?

so sure, you laugh,
think it's all a game, a silly
past time made of candy
colored marbles thrown down
on the four square chalk;
but, I tell you,
I have done these things,
and it is no game;
when done well,
it is a dream. When perfect,
you can be god.

you ever pilot a five hundred ton
robot the height of an office building
across the blasted surface of
a silent white moon?
well, I say, that's where it's at...
poetry in those rockets
squealed through zero g,
the screams of your team mates ejecting...

I have flown Spitfires into visions of hell
the likes of which no one from my generation
will ever be able to imagine,
dog fighting 7 me109s
alone in the skies above
secret missions in the Ardennes...

I have watched entire cities
encapsulated in the protective hull of
capital ships, magisterial sea-cow inheritances
from the British Empire,
shatter in space, their bows broken,
and have heard the screams as everyone was slaughtered.

I have also explored caves. So many caves. More caves
than there are in the known universe... been down every one
and back again
two times or more...

I have fought the black knight,
borne on the back of an ostrich.
I have done that. I have done that.

I have flown through city night skies
a blue serpent, unseeable, secretive,
twisting and serene, like smoke through the skyline.

I have woken to visions of hell so supreme
that only grenades can solve it,
meaty axe monsters, giant, red-balloon demons,
fictions too obscene for any madman, dreams
that inhabit the minds only of the living dead

and yet, I have seen a girl cry,
small and weary, stupidly clutching a doll,
her mother cut down by sniper fire,
and I have wanted to cry as well...

I have seen an ancient old man
long forgotten in the tombs
of a fictional world
after a fictional apocalypse.
Deranged and broken,
they left him there for so long...
but I have heard him!
he sings to the steel,
the walls, and vacuum pressured doors;

he sings ancient songs of vaudeville
that no one else I know
knows or remembers; I write fan letters,
I cry, I get drunk thinking of such things,
for, for once, someone has
managed to envision my future as I see it;
they have encapsulated a future me and
sent me back to me so I can hear,
behind the music;
I can hear the overt message;

I have seen and done these things,
and they were real.
Real enough to dream of.
Good enough to remember for years;
things worth crying over,
experiences that sadden the heart
and exalt the spirit:
standing at sunrise
over a blasted town
or flying home after a long mission when
"flack's opening up;"
jeesus;= my whole wing is dead;
hit the silk, now, get out! and the canopy's jammed...
that's what I have done, forgetting many
other exceptional dreams.
These are the things that I think of
when drunk and in need of another world
so, in the words of that desperate,
last-ditch pilot:
"this one's for you, Gerri"
let him have it.

Flack's opening up...

# BUSHIDO BLADE:

i am Irish Rapier man.
why they let a guijin into the dojo
is a question that I do not need to ask;

I am fighting on the beach at sunset.
my legs made useless by
the crazy russian bitch,
her blonde cavalry saber spinning
reflecting glints of dappled whites
bouncing off the water,
she cuts at tendons in my knees.

i fall, staggered; my blade
drives deep into the endless depth
of the starfish colored sand.

I look up, waiting for the telling blow.
this is my bushido.

or:

I am the master.
dishonored, betrayed;
they are taking everything away from me;

I have only to perform one last act,
though the blood runs in crimson rivers
through my robes, the world a winter cave of
black blank dizzy spells,

a telescope viewed through the wrong end,
I walk bolt upright, the guts
spilling out of me with each step,
my heart a thing now that most cannot fathom;
all my students dead...


...

after it's all over, my debt to duty paid
i lean, pale and gone, against a shrine,
supplicant, in a moment's prayer;
i remove the hidden dagger from my robe
and, with tears stinging cuts on my face (for I would live
my whole lifetime again just to see another day)
I grit my teeth and close my eyes
grunting "THIS is MY BuSHidO..."

so:

Joe and I are going for first to 200 kills;
fucker
figured out how to master blocking.
we cripple each other with
a vast array of melee weapons.
I dishonor myself by
throwing sand in his face,
(have to save the round...)

we scream "NO!" dying
at each-other's hand:
"YOU CHEAP SHIT FUCKER!
            that's RAPE YOU FUCK!"

"Oh, I've never seen *that* move before",
derisive psych-outs amidst the game's
clashing of blades.

we acknowledge moments of the other's exceptional skill,
"I guess I bobbed when I should have weaved,
maybe that would have kept your sword
OUT OF MY FUCKING EYE!" or comment on remarkable
timing; "fucking-a; I HAD you! You Were Dead!
Nice..." drawn out like the last breath of
a punctured lung.

we hit 200, pause, stretch the wrist, exhale.
"One more?"
"Yeah, lets change the map."
and we go again.

**This is my Bushido...**

# CRAZY TAXI:

this is the long drive of attrition
rickshaw fingers
fighting time
struggling for fares;
covering distance
like something with claws
pulling itself along, fiercely
digging into the pavement
a motorized puma driven
by a madman.

After a certain point,
the only thing you want
is to STOP and have a Pepsi,
sit in a dark room
quell the shakes
still the shattered nerves
look at the sun
stare at the beach
take it all in;

but it's not really worth it.
the corporate sponsorships dictate
that you must continue your quest
for 'Crazy Money' so
floor it.
Put that
pedal to the metal
and go.

**YEEHAW!!!!**

## KARNOV:

If I ate fire I should think
That I would be a great man,
Standing there with my
Huge, sweaty breasts,
Shirt off and chest gleaming
As I shoved that glowing ember
Into my throat, leaving the crowd
In a hushed moment of awe
And lilting, idling ecstasy...
And then, without them even
Having the suspicion to wait,
Without them even suspending
Disbelief or adult-like doubt,
I'd blow that giant mass of
Awesome burning loudness
Right out into the center of the ring
And they would applaud me
Because my presentation was
So perfect that they forgot
To expect the inevitable payoff.

## FIRE SHOW:

(Or: Daughter of Karnov)

for Darren and Holli, Superstar Bartenders at Brewske's

*"Not for you, but for me*

*this time."*

*-Charles Bukowski,* HOSTAGE

Scarecrow bartender, Double D'

blows a lit-spit cloud

of Bacardi One-Fifty-One

down the bar.

Man, how it roars, cross

his flaming fingertips, rousing

the startled screams

of the pretty girls,

big, dumb, and bright.

but what really blows my mind

is when little Holli of the big boobs,

pretty face, and sad eyes

takes the floor.

Almost half the height of Double D',

she takes twice the 151

in her soft and beautiful mouth.

she swings her hips subtly,

as if to say, all drunken business, "okey, D',

let's go... let me

show you how it's done."

The weary beauty with the black hair
lights her fingertips
        like It Don't Mean A Thing
                "don't matter if it's sweet or
                hot..."
   full-tilts
              snake-like
          back
and then catapults that
torch ball out like a fucking bullwhip

The applause comes too soon, for,
even as the fireball
is leaving her light red lips,
              with a faint spray of booze
              echoing on the edge of the flaming cloud,

she's leaning back again,
  wiping her mouth with a
  salty, back-a-tha-hand;
she lilts, for just a second,
her body smiling, almost
like Pretty Momma's gonna shake it;
    full of secrets.

Her mouth burning from the antiseptic Bacardi,
she hurls a second ball without waiting.
Sideshow beauty
spits booze onto the floor
like a sailor after a fight.

She smiles sharply,
delighting in her triumph,
and then raises her arms
embracing the hoots and exaltations;
betcha no one thought
she could do that.

She is my Venus.

# KID ICARUS:


My father is the musical director for
a local production of Stephen Sondheim's
latest hit musical, "Company".


This town is still fatally small, but somehow innocent
and the musicians have yet to be crucified.


They've rented two pianos to complement
the one we already own:
they are placed in different rooms
all over the big house, our giant ranch domain
with seventies decor, low ceilings;
ashtrays, lamps that lean in a giant curve of
thin metal sprouting in a tan ceramic shade
that is like the gradient fill of a sunset
or the brown of a brown egg, bulbing upside-down.


the house is packed every night for two weeks with
all of these famous-seeming people;
the vital screeching of women, bear-like guffaws of men;
it's as if the circus has come to town and
set up shop in my living room.
I know they are doing something great.


the normal logic of life has been suspended,
upended; altered, shifted like the magazines and ashtrays on
a table overturned by a party driven mad with the
obsessive desire to play Monopoly;
anything to set up the board.

Because of this war-time law, my mother allows me
to stay up till midnight; I am eight and
doing this without having to conceal my offence is a thrill.

I am allowed this freedom with one condition:
I must stay in The Pit;
The Pit; my playroom; a room sunken four feet below
the rest of the living room, with high walls
and wood columns at the top;  the
walls are lined with red shag carpeting;
this is my universe...
being "sentenced" to The Pit is like convicting
a junky and shipping him off to do time in
a shooting gallery.

The Pit has no real door; just a small gate up to the waist,
and I can hear all that goes on in the house above.
My father is working, training singers; they split up
each night, into different rooms of the house,
boys and girls divided, like the stories I hear in Hebrew school
about the way the orthodox worship;
there is always singing from this point on,
singing, part writing, adjustment, "fuck" drawled at times,
mostly laughter, and always joy... I hear
this all, delighted, these voices from
"the above world"
these people, who, somehow, love what they are doing,
are coming together in a way that I still can't envision;
all brotherhood and hard work fellowship of
the show jazz jive, a sacrament sewn deep within me,
maybe, right there; saying "hang in there, Seth;
one day, there will be life... it is possible."

And every night, for at least five hours, sometimes
more, I sit in the darkened Pit,
listening to every motherfucking word of every fucking song
and every cue for every pickup bar
and every combination of quartet for "Sorry/Grateful"
until, eventually, I know the words by heart
(including the difficult patter songs)
and, while listening, I play Kid Icarus;
I am The Winged One,
looking like a gay ass cupid in a tennis skirt
with his orange-ish face framed by the brown wood facade
of the TV that I sit too close to...
I shoot my arrows for weeks, mastering all;
every irritating jump, every surreal scene of
quasi-underworld ruin and Greek and Roman pseudo imagery,
every utterly bizarre abstract blue devil harpy enemy
flying to assault me; my feet carrying me into ascension.

Then, one night, I played into the early morning;
it was two before my mother came to get me,
with the last of the show people muttering out,
lingering around the door of the house,
discussing things with dad;
I protested with much zeal; "I'm at the end of the game!"
I whispered, hissing, dejected.
My mother wasn't getting it,
writing off my accomplishment as being a stupid kid thing:
"But I've played all this time to get where I am now..."
I said, tired, watching the last of the singers
filter out into the early desert night, the wilderness
surrounding our outpost at Rainbow and Sahara;

"They're almost done too," my mother said,
"the show is almost ready for opening night; that's why you
got to stay up so late. Now time for bed."

this was before codes really worked;
back when you would spend an hour trying to decipher
the significance of a blurry blob of pixels in Metroid
muttering in your mind ridiculous questions like
"is that an 'o' or a cap or Arab A?"
only to find that, no matter what, after writing
all possible combinations of the blue gibberish
down on a piece of scrap paper,
that the result did not work, and that you had inevitably lost it all...

so, that night, I left the game on, TV off;
somehow I woke up early the next morning
and got thirty minutes
of the game in me before school...
I was lost in a maze... a terrible
vertical, horizontal maze,
all made of blue and black stone;
all so complicated... even if I had had the patience
I would never have found the time to map it,
to work it all out on paper, figuring
the turns I missed, the mistakes that led me
to dead ends or fierce fire pits of monsters;

as Nana started the car to go,
early chill of winter, sitting there in
my school clothes,
I somehow knew that I had gone too far,

and that to go any further would be impossible;
would be a negation of the going,
an affront to the distance

so, humming the words to "Barcelona" in my head
I turned off the console;
my winged faggot with the huge head and the tennis
skirt packed away his bow and arrow the right way,
in the early morning, after surviving the long
lonesome night in the heart of the maze,
probably subsisting on worms and roots until
I obliterated his universe, sucked
the life spark from his stupid fucking shoes,
sent him plummeting to his doom, feet clad in clumps
of melted wax
and never played the game again.

still, I think that was one of the happiest moment of my life
for I had made a choice; I chose not to pursue, desperately,
that which was unreachable, in favor of
creating the raw memory of a journey unfulfilled.
I did not need to go any higher. I had gotten what I came for
so I quit, just as the day found itself dawning,
the sun spreading its misery through the ice kissed wind
taunting the flightless world of man.

**Icarus' Ascent Into Heaven**

## PAPERBOY:

if only I could save you
from the blondes in the black
Duesenbergs; hold you back,
grab your fucking handle-bars,
shaking my head, preventing
your insane ride into traffic
saying "it's not worth it, kid;
whatever they're paying you,
it's not worth it."

## SINISTAR:


Your voice was so loud and bleak
hyped up and amped by hardware
that I would turn around
to check that you were not coming for me
in reality.

BEWARE: I LIVE@!@!
I don't know why I ever played you,
it scared the shit out of me so much,
knowing that you would come for me,
swooping as a punishment
a savage monstrous thing
a psychotic bully the size of a planet...

      (now, when I play you on emulators,
      you seem like such a psychotic thought problem:
      why the fuck am I collecting gems in space
      if there is this thing, this
      skull-head face with steel rims
      and hair-band 80's spikes?
      why would I ever choose to live again
      when the only outcome is for you to destroy me?)

BEWARE: I HUNGER@!@!
knowing that there is no escape,
the star field bordered by the screen;
no way to run away; I must perform my functions
quickly; must stave the inevitable with
stop gaps... until, suddenly,

DIE@!@DIE@!@DIE!@DIE!@DIE@!DIE@!DIE!:
holy shit; and I am screaming like a little girl
as you fill the screen with your bouncing madness;
you beat the shit out of my ship,
smashing me over and over again like
a prizefighter gone insane after a fight,
kicking and crushing his opponent's head in,
your jaw flapping in your frenzy,
my little jets can't take me away; it is a nightmare.
I wheel and shoot but its pointless; you're invincible, unstoppable,
and always just fast enough to be too fast for me; you scream,
I scream; the space blackness fills my lungs, freezing me like a
flavor crystal, vacuum turns me into glass as the cockpit shatters;
you shake, pulsating, a vortex of bone, and my ship spins, out
of sync; now just driftwood, dwindling down the drain of your
mouth.

god, I loved that game.

**Run, Coward! RUN!**

## 3D:

I still hate it; they took
the platformers away,
robbed my Contra heroes
of their bitter destinies;
survival in a world ruled by
aliens and robots; everything destroyed...
shot both the red and blue guy
from every two player in the head
and left them to die without
character, explanation, or reason;
I don't think they understood it at the time,
but the art was going out of everything,
abstract symbol with significance 'x'
was being replaced with "new flashy thing
that seems more real 'y'"

their ghosts whisper to me, though,
from their /dev/null oblivion graves,
begging for their quests to reach fulfillment
or, at least, for a too-tired kid
to hit the power button;
"but we came through so much... why now?" they cry.
there is no answer.

**Generic Sidescrolling Shooter**

## SHAREWARE:


before modems hit the scene,
I would purchase brightly illustrated
Apogee cardboard packets
crammed with 3 and a half inch floppies
for five to ten bucks
and play my brains out
on the demos.

This was how I first knew Doom
and Duke Nukem
and Commander Keene (if memory serves).

I keep them stacked neatly in a box
as if waiting for their owner to return.
I don't know why,
but they feel special to me, like
a photo album from my childhood, pages
filled with faces of relatives
that I never really knew.

# DOOM:

I would so hate
to have been this space marine
who, after kissing his wife
goodbye,
set off on a mission
to Phobos; "see you later, honey!"
The fool! The poor fool!

# QUAKE:

everything fresh and new,
screaming down my brand new
56k modem; mods! Guys!:
We Can Change The Game!
crush it, break it, remake it
in our own image; redefine
the physics, draw new bounds,
make new worlds: WHOLE NEW WORLDS
in which to fight and kill and die.
New weapons, gadgets,
toys, tricks, traps, anything;
with an SDK and a dream, the
engine becomes a canvas of
death and battle for every 14 year old
whose got the guts to read a
FAQ or a manual or a README;
this is revolution.
this is the future.

this is now.

## LAG:

I fire three grenades into the hall,
turn to flee before the five guys
on the other team, armed with nail
guns and rocket launchers, are
able to hit me with deflecting fire
and splash damage from around the
corner, when, suddenly,

        I am
    mo
            v   i   n   g   throughtimethat
wo  rks  li          ke              liquid
and then flows like tap water or mo
    la
            s
              s
        e
            s
(hoping, praying, that the server doesn't time me out;
come on you fucking packets, move! get down that
wire; hoping that I'm not alone; if it's just me
and not the entire server I am sure to wake up dead;
coming out of the slow time to the score screen,
respawning with a pistol and a lot of fear; maybe
happening multiple times) b    ut
the                 slow
    time    stops and I'm happy because all my
keystrokes during the fat chunk of lag seem to have
saved my life; you have to take preemptive measures

like hiding; moving while not moving, telling your
character to do things you cannot see; the screen
a frozen shot of a time that has already passed; a
portrait of a never-ending now that is really already a
then; other players still moving, flowing through
normal time see me as a statue, grenade launcher
raised, pointing to the ceiling,
standing by the staircase; they'd probably laugh
and frag me, spraying the room with some
rockets, knowing that I am not, in fact,
where I appear to be, because, you see,
I am, in fact, moving; even though I am frozen
in place like a military figurine, a grim
toy soldier made to represent a fighter in a
worthless hypothetical war.

In truth, I have already left this room
(because I know the map better than
I know my own house and can measure things
by time and keystrokes,
precision approximations for a blind man lost
in a world without tactile sensation), and have
already put away my grenade launcher, drawn
the grappling hook, and (provided no one killed
me on my way), am now hanging above the entryway
to the subterranean castle, a happy little camper
hoping to god I didn't get it in the silent wormhole
vacuum, where time no longer corresponds to movement.

All of this, however, has, at once, occurred, but not
yet happened; after my connection chews and swallows
the reality gap that is the lag, it will be like a switch
has been thrown and I will suddenly perform

all of the actions I have just described, but
will perform them all instantaneously. Most of them
will occur in sequence, but a few will likely happen before
the one that preceded it (always sucks when you
put the grenades away and fire what you think
is a machine gun only to find that you were
still firing grenades and are now going to die
because you have filled a room with the little
lighted canisters; pipe bomb suicide).

When the lag has passed, I will fly around the level,
insane, seemingly out of control, like the Flash.
a murderous psychopath springboarding around
a texture mapped castle like a spitball shot
from a rubber band. I sigh, impatiently;
I was having a good run.
I sit and pray to the god of servers, modems,
and phone lines while waiting to see if I am still alive,
already hungry to kill again.

## MEDITATIONS ON MURDER:
## (for Raiden)

*"Jack, you were the best to come out of the eighties; the other kids in your regiment even had a name for you... What was it? Ah, I remember... Jack The Ripper... What went wrong, Jacky-Boy?"*
–Solidus Snake, Metal Gear Solid: Sons of Liberty

while killing sentries atop
the oil derrick,
I wonder if these men possess
the capacity to love; if they have dreams
of anything other than this.

I shoot one in the face,
appearing from behind a corner
silently, just a whisper
of the sea, buddy, just a whisper of the sea.

"I was a North American Fall Webworm in my former life. Those were the good old days. What were you in your former life?"
-The Colonial, Metal Gear Solid: Sons Of Liberty

## MARIO IN EXILE:

*"I AM PLANNING GREAT THINGS!"*
the drunken Italian dictator shouts,
legs extended, like Stalin
in repose before the fireplace,
lost in books and leather and the madness
of dreams gone wrong.

He laughs, suddenly,
a dark, cold, merciless laugh of
brutal irony, joyless mirth; reminiscent of
gulag exemptions denied,
of punks murdered with axes in the street.

He throws the brandy snifter against the wall.
*"GREAT THINGS!"* he roars,
reiterating his main premise to the empty room...
the resultant silence replaced by a soft chuckle,
dead in the air, muffled
by the books and the leather.

"Where is the music?" he mumbles, humming
the theme from his first great campaign... trails off, then silence.
he stares at the Persian rug, lost inside himself
and begins tweaking his mustache,
the one thing that remains vibrant
on his craggy face;
well-waxed and black as sin,
the life-energy of the land absorbed
in those hairs;

"GReat things," he whispers, drooling, in hiccup,
a smile rudely stretched across his face,
souring into grimace...

he does not call for the princess
for she is dead, turtle shell in the head;
self-inflicted, found clutching a note with one question:
"where has my plumber gone?"

**Great Things...**

## HALF-LIFE:


I have a crowbar
and many problems;

      apparently, I wasn't
      working on what I had thought;
      a new toothpaste, a better mousetrap;
      through science, anything is possible.

Thank The Man In The Blue Suit.
      set us all up. I curse his name
      while crawling through the shattered red
      of the broken reactor core.

    ...


what is a crowbar?
a hook on some metal, a stick
a split; you'd
be surprised
      what someone
    with a crowbar and
the will to live can do;
      amazing things;

it feels good in my hand.
      I flip it, loose, while
      walking through the halls,
      admiring its blunt weight.

relaxed in my hand,
        it almost seems
                to float.


...


Things aren't so good
for me lately.


II.
the aliens have come.
        Ha! I never thought I would say that;
        never believed in them
                until now.

biology is a remarkable science.
You come to admire it
while smashing head crabs
or killing
        the co-workers
they have converted.

    I can't lie.
I am very afraid.


III.
these things with the tongues,
I really hate them.

Bulbous gut bags
> drooling  a slithering thermometer;
> a subtle pink python, glistening,
> dangling from the ceiling, dying
> to encircle you, and
> pull you into its jaws.

> once, while out of ammo, I
> had to let it catch me; had
> to prepare myself, knowing; crowbar
> at the ready, my body quaking,
> fearful of the fall. I
> had to step into the tongue; had
> to embrace it.
> shiver.

> thirty feet up to the ceiling, I
> rode that sticky-slime gym rope,
> staring into the toothy hole
> from which it emanated.
> I thought of nothing but the crowbar, and,
> when I could smell the creature's decay,
> could see its gelatinous organs pulsing,
> I swung and jammed, sharp end out, never
> making a sound, while
> wetting my pants.

> It died and the rope went slack and
> I fell to the floor
> along with the chunky rain
> of the thing's inner meat.

Fun day at the office.

Afterwards,
I used the crowbar to smash boxes
like a rape victim, crying,
only partly to look for health.

Still, the crowbar was with me.
At least I had that.

IV.
Even after I had gotten a whole arsenal
of better weapons – automatic rifles,
crossbows, missile launchers, grenades,
deagles, and, yes, even that disgusting
alien weapon that fired the homing bugs
(I could never hold one in my hand; its
little legs squirming, the waterbug shell
on its backside unnaturally smooth against
my suit gloves; fuck this, I'd think,
feeding it back into the gun that dispensed it; I'll
stick to grenades), even
after I had all of these guns, I still loved
the simple beauty of the crowbar the best.

The other weapons jammed, or left me with an
empty clip in the face of a horde of multi-eyed
red slime people from hell; with the crowbar,
at least I knew I could make a go of
hacking my way through them… anything was possible
with it in my hands.

...

indeed, at times of doubt, while jumping
from a broken catwalk shakily suspended
over a fifty foot drop into
a tank of green toxic goo, I
would often pull out the crowbar
just to make myself feel better, just
to make sure I could do it, will my feet
forward... each step, a heart attack.

V.

So, by the time the military showed up
I just laughed; somehow,
it didn't seem to matter that they were there
to kill me as well. Security, after all, is
everyone's responsibility.

in truth, I actually
enjoyed seeing them die;
their corpses being blown back
from behind boxes by
something horrible, or
being sucked into the ceiling
by the tongue bags, or
being converted by the head crabs;
it all reeked of "been there, done that."
I would lean back on my rifle
and watch, whistling, under my breath;
"tactics, guys; you gotta use tactics"
I'd wait till they were all dead
and then clean up the corners with
my crowbar. The Janitor Of The Damned.

...

I had no problem killing them.
They were just doing their jobs,
sure, sure; but
I was just doing mine. Sometimes,
at night now, I do get angry; the cocksuckers...

just the sad betrayal of it, the first time
their guns swung around to me,
"SURRENDER FREEMAN!" my heart
sank
in a horrible new way.

after I realized they were killing everyone,
though, I enjoyed making them die.
A surgeon with a shotgun, I'd carve them up;
a room exploding around me; just more fucking
meat that had to be killed; just more fucking
problems to solve. No reasons. No science
to it at all. Just meat. Just problems.

...

the only time I let myself truly hate the soldiers
was when they had me pinned down in a sewer.
they exhibited a vile cunning that
separated them from the aliens; grenades
clanking down into my steel foxhole,
I cursed them all to hell and
then sent them to it.

Of course, it is debatable if I could send them
to a place worse than where we were, but,
by that point, I was beginning to feel at home
with it all. Humans are a highly adaptable species;
we can get used to anything. Anything.

Day turned to night, and I sat in a small room
doubting God with every
fiber of my being while
waiting for a sleep which never came.


VI.
As disturbing as Black Mesa had been,
the alien planet was oddly soothing.
No head crabs, just one Big Ugly Thing
I had to kill.
even though I cheated (used all the codes)
I couldn't figure out how to beat the thing.
So, eventually, I saved and gave up.

even after quitting the game
I still wanted to shake
The Man In The Blue Suit.
he ruined my whole day, and
sometimes, I still want to know
Why.

## THE MEGA MAN HAIKUS:


CUTMAN:
scissor-headed freak
white lunatic suit squeeze hands
and crushed face: chop! chop! chop!
you are absurd

GUTSMAN:
no one knows why, guts;
why the name, guffawing prick.
why the helicopters?...
tedious map.

WILEY:
I am one gun with
one arm and no purpose but
to blow your white fro
wig from your head

(ROBOTNICK)
float, Wiley's sex pal
rocket propelled bubble bitch
invented the mech-squirrel;
a fierce creation!

ICEMAN:
make your dumb platforms
disappear at intervals
your ice gun will be mine
shivers in the cold

MEGAMAN:
you always shout yay!
every motion so fiercely
popping, gay, blue jumpsuit
gun-arm in air.

## A GOOD WALK SPOILED:
## (A toast to games with the personality of cardboard)


The ability to walk
from one side of the screen
to the other
smashing enemies with
your two, totally impractical,
yet completely unblockable,
martial arts moves
is a common character in my memory.

It staggers into my consciousness occasionally,
like an extra from a Lego commercial
directed by bloodthirsty retarded hipster children;
Stab him, YEAH! Jump! COOOOL!!! AGAIN! AGAIN!
AGAIN!

The dull brawl and tough, solemn procession
from left to right, left to right,
goes on and on
level after level
fighting the same goddamned enemies
from fifteen seconds before;
goons dressed in bright colors, as if
they were costumed by Broadway queens
intent on making them members
of the chic-est gang ever.

The cast is the same;
sometimes a guy with a knife or

molotov cocktail or a gunman,
(whose firearm flashes and blinks
before disappearing after being defeated),
peppered with the occasional robot
like roadside signs flitting by amongst
the endless sea of fist-boys and kick-girls
who rise to challenge you.

The echoes of The Story remain constant.
Just as the gameplay never varied,
(Up to jump, press "a" to punch)
the characters lived with one shared and
universally shabby identity, each
interchangeable and pointless, born
into a backstory that read like some 8-year old's
pretense at creating a reason for action figures to fight:

There's always the girlfriend.
There's always the ransom note.
There's always the communication from the kidnappers.
(either on TV, hidden in the classified ads, or
just a simple phone call);
        always a simple, stupid message,
        always in CAPS:
        "WE GOT YOUR DAUGHTER! HA HA HA!"
...     Jesus, the lack of creativity was astounding.

Starting way back in the old days
(when raster graphics still seemed so new)
the genre was spawned by games like "Vigilante"...
        (skinheads have kidnapped Madonna;
        time to go to work!)

Continued
Into the eighties and nineties
with 64th Street, a rip off of a rip off that would be
ripped off by Final Fight;
Zoot Suit or bare chest, everyone's ass
still gets kicked.

Christ, it got so that the thought of one more quarter
would send shudders down your spine, the
"CONTINUE?" screen becoming a real challenge; a dare, a
test of your capacity for enduring
endless and unvaried repetition... over and over and over;
we played them
over and over and over
each time, letting the timer run a little further on
before relenting, disgustedly throwing
our quarters back in...
10... CONTINUE?
10... CONTINUE?
9... CONTINUE?
7... CONTINUE?
8... CONTINUE?
5... CONTINUE?
5... CONTINUE?
3... CONTINUE?
2... CONTINUE?
1... CONTINUE?
...WHY?
...WHY?!
TURN IT OFF! TURN IT OFF!

They kept coming, until, eventually, we stopped;

we got a hold of ourselves, shook off
the spell; "What the fuck am I doing!? This
is never going to end! Fuck this!"
But the damage was done; the money made,
the coin collector arrived each week
to harvest the silver river from the machine's guts.
And, in that sense, we all, really, were
the same. No move different, no destiny unique,
no identity
at all.

# SMOKING LIGHT GUNS:

I
(Time Crisis II)

standing bolt upright
in the bowling ally arcade,
I light a cigarette, lift
my foot off the pressure plate
and throw myself into the fray.

my plastic gun recoils and kicks
as I nail the four gunmen
in the china store.
More rappel in from some impossible
place above; there is no skylight.
I kill them too, and return my lighter
to my vest pocket.

little kids watch me like I'm a God.
a chorus of tiny whispers has gathered
behind me; they've never seen anything like
this. Mr. Satan Man in Black three piece suit
totally unstoppable; has got mad skills.

I put on a little show, saying nothing;
a demonstration, if you will; I make it through
the second level (the one with the mad
scrambling onslaught of speed boats)
without missing. once.

Somehow, they are unimpressed; no eye
for subtlety.

So I break my "one in the head instead
of twelve in the body" rule
and unload into anyone who opposes me.
The wows return as I execute
a forest's worth of ninjas.

even though I am eventually killed
by a green beret (snuck up to the screen
and slashed my face with a sword),
they still avert their eyes when I pass,
whispering like a chain gang,
minds glowing, little lives alight with murderous possibilities.


II
(From The Hip)

we have taken Angee, the queen of the café,
the goddess of the scene,
out with us on a hunt for Mary K's Saturday Night
Mirth.

we play House of The Dead.
Despite my best efforts
to keep her alive (a forever dwindling
player 2) her brains get eaten early on.
I continue, unperturbed
and she hangs around to watch.

we begin talking about the cafe,
how much we both love and hate it.

I fight off a school of zombie flying fish
while digging for a smoke
then begin the hunt for my zippo;
somewhere around my waist, deep
in a vest pocket, my gun tilted down,
I am half prostrate before the screen,
still talking as if nothing is going on.
I find the light, pause, flick the flame
into the darkness, take a drag, looking
at her, smiling, thinking this is what
Saturday nights are supposed to be,

I snap the zippo shut,
blue pistol in my left hand now
pointed at the floor
and enjoy the moment, relish
the ZiB ZAB! BOFF! Lights
and sounds, the
roar, in the black gloom
of the last real arcade in Vegas.

I suck it all in like
a charge punch; save it
for a more desperate time
that I'm sure is
yet to come. I save
the Sega GT machines, Top Skater,
Soul Calibur; I suck it like a smoke
after a movie, pull it all in

and let it go.

and then, as if I knew it was coming,
I flinch back at the screen - a microsecond;
merely a glance; a blink, a sneeze, a tick -
and shoot two zombies in the head
all in the same time that it would take you
to curl your trigger finger
an 8th of an inch.

Angee is aghast;
I would have been, too, had I been her;
what I just did
was
impossible.

I shrug like we're in a lighthearted sitcom.

I did once beat the game.
That has to count for something.

# DRAGON'S LAIR:

I remember when Marble Madness first came out,
Preceded by Gauntlet, with "Blue Wizard is about to Die!"
And, "Use potions to Kill Death!" Helpful instructions
Meant to simplify a deadly maze of stone and skeletons,
Where four friends would gather together to search for a
Black square tile, representing a hole that took you
Out of whatever deathtrap hell you were in, and into
The maw of one even deeper and more dangerous than the last.

I remember the syncopated early FM synthesis strains of
The Ikari Warriors bassline, boom chickaboom chickaboom
Chicka didlydumdedum, with 8bit drums kicking in
Relentlessly behind it on the beach, in red or blue
Bandana, or even at the steel encased end of the game:
there was no other music.

But the game I remember most vividly from my childhood
Was less of a game than an emotive experience, a vision of
Struggling heroism: hopeless, sword in hand and
impenetrable jawline,
A scowl forever souring there under a confounded brow and
Crusader's skull cap. The voice would boom out from duel
Stereo speakers (the first game I remember being this loud)
Like the last digitized remnant of carnie talkers
And sideshow barkers,
Preserved inside this small machine, this made up midway...
His voice would reach out to anyone within earshot, announcing:
DRAGON'S LAIR!

With some kind of flourish and tremendous music,
Dirk would drop in from somewhere above, all

Colored cartoon candy stereotype action and overactive animation,
And the voice would continue, setting up the story
Before you even dropped a dime in the machine.
It was stunning, back then; a shocking marvel,
Incomprehensible and flashy and garish and yet somehow perfect,
Even though it was tasteless, much like the first Zoot Suiter...
Something there cried out for respect, said
"BEHOLD! I am a REVELATION!"
The great and terrible rolled into one thing
and dropped at your door...
(Films like The Magic Tollbooth and Excalibur only enhanced
this sense of awe)
But there he was, Dirk, sword in hand, chain mail and orange jerkin,
While the Don Pardo huge voice man sucked at your soul,
willing you to the machine...

It was always that voice and the vision of Dirk
Falling from one thing into another, sword flailing reflexively,
As fifty tentacles attacked;
Each scene set up so simply:
A gigantic cartoon castle of evil that loomed in the distance,
Moat and drawbridge down waiting to encircle our fated hero,
Witless but willing, all so simple and pure
but the first step set the deadly trap in motion,
some sort of evil god inside of every element of the place,
set and bent and waiting to destroy you: DRAGON'S LAIR!
the voice would boom,
And before you knew it you were pumping quarters
into the thing like a mad monkey addicted to cocaine...
no care in the world until there was nothing left.

When you're eight and not easily impressed,
The impressive things that you discover

are not just amazing, but profound;

to the core of your being, you are touched, as was I, by this

spinning multicolored digital analogue whirlygig, this

Immense superstructure that always loomed before me

to the point where, even after I was broke and penniless I would lurk

by the machine,

watching its teaser screen over and over again, transfixed.

It was but a whisper of what was yet to come,

and what, somehow, would never be again.

**Dirk The Daring**

# MARIO VS. THE PUNK ROCK HERO:

I was playing the machine in the
lonesome 7-11 at the corner
of the vast vacant lot that
was my neighborhood, stretching
as far as the eye could see,
forever, out west.

It was the glorious hard core eighties
and I had not yet gotten a nintendo
because they had yet to be invented.

My father was playing a slot machine,
the clerk was tired. It was night,
a deep early night, the kind
only found in childhood, drunk stupors spent
in foreign towns, or discovered
after car accidents.

A punk came in, the real thing;
the first I ever saw in male form;
blue mohawk, the kind that takes a
year to grow, wearing leather jacket
and a belt of chain.

He went to the beverage section,
and, just as he was putting the
40 in his pants,
I happened to turn from the machine to look at him.

I don't know what made me turn around;
maybe it was because he was directly
behind me and I was afraid
he would eat me (I really was scared of them;
they looked scary. They still do).

He did the truest thing, then, the
thing that made me like punks for
the rest of my life.
Instead of knifing me, causing a scene,
or releasing a howling rage which would
summon his gang of monstrous freaks,
born on the backs of harleys, and ordering them
to raze the place with me and my father still inside it,
he held his finger up to his lips,
pants unzipped, silently struggling
the big bottle into his whitey tighties...
I think it was Old E...
(still one of the funniest and most fucked up memories of my
childhood...
punk with 40 in pants,
manically gesturing a call for max sneakitude...)

I nodded in assent, understanding.

I looked for only a second more, filled with
wonder at the courage of this vibrant thief;
this daring psycho, who, Solid Snake-like
crept in under the wire of the guard-eyes
of authority, grown weary with the day's work
and welcoming the cool leisure of the night,
deflating lazily into the haze of nine pm...

he arrived silently, making what he wanted most
into a reality by any means necessary, but,
rather than kill us all, he moved with stealth...

despite being discovered, caught, red-handed
(by the most troublesome variable, a child,
one who was likely to reveal him with a sneeze,
or an intake of breath, sharp; huh! rousing the alarm, or
just with the dumb whimper of a kid) -

he held true, and trusted life,
giving me the high sign, hoping
with his pants down, not to be undone by
a five year old.

I went back to my game, looking away,
aware of the way energy shifts in a room,
generating suspicion, or the fatal
curious turn of the head; I did not wish
such a fate on a ninja so honorable;
this Bushido-Blade Beer Thief.

I returned to the asinine jumping into tubes and
squashing goombas in all their orange
"I'm a weird grumpy mushroom walking; please kill me!"-splendor.

I felt the air displace beside me
as he made for the door,
mission accomplished; fading forever into the anonymous night...
Sauntering, cocky, secure,
         everything I could never be.

I lived and died many times that night,
but I didn't really care about Mario and his stupid cartoon energy;
his hopeless quest seemed banal to me in the context
of what I had just seen; I wanted to steal a fucking beer.

I threw him into pits dumbly,
let him be crushed carelessly by turtle shells that he himself
had brought into the universe... he was no
Legend of Kage leaping through trees,
he was no punk. He was
just a fucking plumber out to kill the guy who
took his chick...

it was my first inkling of dumb dreams gone horribly wrong,
a subtle hint left by life, a preparatory note
for the fucked up reality that would be my life
in Vegas, my kid journey through the digital eighties;
I found myself hungry for anarchy.

# JOUST:

i don't think there is much doubt that riding an ostrich
is pretty gay, especially when done as some part of a
renaissance festival gone
horribly
horribly
wrong;
but gliding on those wings, those feeble orange and yellow wings,
in the caverns and crumbling ledges in the torchlight
fighting those frantic feathered foes,
assaulting each other with such great speed that,
after a certain level,
it was impossible to tell what was happening;
the whole thing degenerating into a mad
pixelized scramble of swirling color,
everything a frantic clutching dash;
a final assault, with no room for mistakes,
just the frantic tapping of the big red button, trying to gain leverage
just one more... one more and

knocked off, the black knight approaches.
The Time Keeper; the killer of the incompetent
in the early levels, appearing now as
the executioner of those who have played
for far too long,
showing up like the game company's
personal hit-man, sent to take you out;
            "time for this one to make room for the
            other kiddies; get them hooked as well..."

        (no wonder Tron was such a hit;
                back in those days, the MCP
                        really did exist,
                        a corporate entity composed
                        of game company built-in
                        configurability merged with
                        greedy arcade owners)

so, it all comes to this, you,
on your ass, feebly fumbling for
the lance; where the fuck is that bird?
not in the lava? not possible... (stunned, killed so many...
failed to notice the gray hand of the lava troll
claiming your trusted steed, dragging it
down into the magma soup; bird screams echoing
off the walls...)
it seems such a waste:
everyone dead; insanity! for whom do they fight?
what feudal lord is supposed to be
sitting in your position, on the other side of the screen?

the clicking hooves of the black knight's
demon ostrich bang like gavels on your guts
as he canters slowly towards you,
with those fucked up white eyes,
like something totally alien lives behind the shell of his human form,
his blue silhouette;

he says nothing... does nothing to acknowledge
the exceptional circumstances surrounding his summoning...
does not even remark about your high score;
the highest he's ever seen...

none of it matters to this kill switch;

and, in a fit of madness in which the
crude system of significances of the game
take hold of the player,
after hours of struggling, during this single game,
hours of battling winged enemy after enemy,
scrambling across the disintegrating cave floor
screaming, close calls too many to count,
from this combat weariness... this war-hardening,
the player is somehow magically conjoined
with the character he controls; for the first time
the consequences of his actions are written out
in a flash; the gibbering boggle of the game
is set down and put to reason, like a memoir,
in that exceptional instant
the user sees himself in the soul of the code...
part of the program in every sense.

it is for this reason that the dismounted player
does not move, makes no attempt to flee
from the otherworldly demon that now approaches him;
each step seems to whisper "this is how they all end, eventually"
there's no use;

the transfigured player
watches as his character, exhausted from the battle,
heaving, on one arm, legs splayed beneath him,
the lance just inches out of reach,
becomes suddenly calm
and prepares himself for the death blow
by smiling like he's seeing all the dreams in heaven
even as he's executed in this volcanic hell:

for he knows that others have never come so far
and his name will live on for months to come
singing of his valiant accomplishments
whenever the scoreboard flashes his initials
right there at the top
five seconds at a time.

**We can be heroes...**

## INTERESTING CONCEPT:

first of all, it must be said
that the titles were almost always universally horrible:
"Streets of Rage", "Faxanadu", "Bayou Billy"...
ARKANOID: Revenge of DOH
... I mean, what the fuck does the title
"Space Harrier" have to do
with running across an endless
field for eternity, shooting gigantic centipedes?

I guess it's the fault of the story; usually,
there isn't one; especially in the good old days...

"so, um, why am I killing all these people with this tank?"
or
"Ok, I get the premise that I am in a helicopter,
but, why is it called a Tiger Heli, and
why am I destroying civilian targets?"
or, the best of all:
"why am I the only guy fighting this war?
what, they expect one guy to take out an entire army?"
    the answer is, of course, yes.

plots aside, my favorite games, it must be noted,
were the ones that predated, to a large extent,
even the penultimate sophistication of
the side scrolling shooter, with its
endlessly repeating backgrounds,
tedium of jumps, and infinite ammo...

no, I look most fondly on the games
where the actual logic of them is not apparent;
so abstract
that they form a universe of nonsensical dreams,
out of a sparse, vector-drawn, 3-color symbology...

Tempest; a game in which you are embodied
by a prong shaped like a boomerang,
a sentry set atop a 3 dimensional tube
shooting down at the advancing enemies...
oh, look! I killed another red x thing...
or the aforementioned ARKANOID:
look, what the fuck is this game about;
where is there any "revenge" in
breaking bricks by bouncing a ball
off a paddle? and the paddle is supposed to be my ship?
I'm in the fucking ping pong paddle? What the fuck?

those were the days
when a game was a thing meant to augment the imagination;
there was usually no plot line, no goal but to score big points,
rarely a story of any kind;
what kind of narrative history can a
character that is represented as a single white line
ever hope to posses? none.

the lure here was to witness the beauty of the game,
games the likes of which the world
had never really known; games in which
the board was limited only by
the technical wizardry of the programmers
and the processing and display limitations of the hardware...

because of this, my memory is riddled with
remembrances of games in which a person
is flung into a maze of death and forced to run
from an incontrovertible and unavoidable
creature; a horrible monster, spawned
from the darkest madness within the human heart;
fleeing is made the soul point of the game,
running from death for the rest of your life...
bizarre...

but then there were games that presented you with
a totally unique universe of their madness,
in which you were caught, trapped,
suddenly enchanted by the dictum of the
open-ended gameplay; the impossibly silly
aspects no longer mattered; you got hooked,
working it...

these games were the only form of art
in human history which was neither
beautiful nor criticized for their crudity,
was not flashy, academic,
or part of the mainstream populist
identity; these games were art
that you experienced; a moving formalism,
a type of aesthetic dance or movement drama
for the clutzy geeks, the desperate jerks,
and the punk kids of my generation;

whereas real towns had community theater,
sports, better schools, and established identities,
We had arcades.

sure, there was some vague appeal
to the notion of destroying things
without fear of retribution, but
for me, there was the beauty of the game; it shone
through far beyond anything else...
everything so bear and simple and all right there in front of you
yet making so little sense, intuitive, obtuse and overt,
splashed of 8 bit colored lines against a forever screen
of absolute black... there, in my own reflection, I would find truths
that would sustain me for the rest of my life;
intoxicating lessons that I would carry with me to me grave,
cause I know for sure
that it wasn't all the flash that kept me coming back.

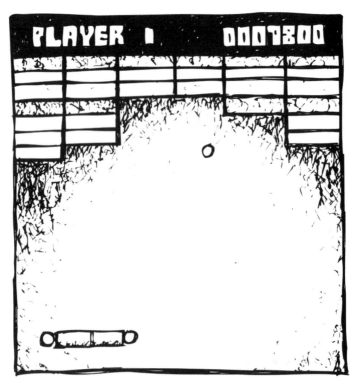

**Generic Arkanoid Clone**

# A VERY SPECIAL MESS AGE FROM MAJOR HAVOC:

I
AM
Major Havoc;
my clone armies chart
the progress of my
Catastrofighter as
i battle the dreaded
alien scourge;

I am humanity's last
hope.

CLONED by the scientists,
I am a devious, space-bound
saboteur. My life's mission
is financed by
an eight year-old child.

TOGETHER,
      (With his quarters and my
      endlessly rapacious appetite
      for excitement and adventure)
WE will bring an end
to the eons of tyranny
that have held us down and
made us subservient to the
vicious alien conquerors.

AND:
If I die, know that
there are many more
behind me, just like me,
(in fact, just more me's)
who are more than willing
to do their duty.

All from one, one from all!

## ASTROSMASH:
## (For The Blue Sky Rangers)


BEHOLD!:
The Glorious REvOluTiON HAS BEGUN!

Sit and play FOREVER.
Why would you ever stop?
Controls so silky smooth,
pulsing tick of fuzz time,
unending kamikaze asteroids
pelting your new high score;

By four in the morning,
you will be blind
psychotic
exhausted
and happy.

Sitting alone in the darkened den
you will grudgingly shut the system down
only to sit and think
of playing the game
before reluctantly going to bed
where you will dream
of asteroids
and chase, in sleep, the next
harder level.

## MISSILE COMMAND:

It is a great irony
that a child
tortured by fears
of nuclear holocaust
should take such delight
in a game
that gave its own
programmer
nightmares
of the apocalypse;
      the mushroom cloud
          rising as a splash
      of red pixels,
          the dream maker
tortured
      by his own creations.

Meanwhile,
I lose the last base:
blew my missiles too early,
panicked; couldn't
pace myself "My God, we're
all going to die," I thought,
and we did.

The Game Over screen comes up
and, with sweaty palms
I whisper one word, standing
in awe of the end
of life as we know it:
"heavy…"

fun game.

## BUBBLE BOBBLE:

Bub and Bob
get da banana!
ICE CREAM! Explode
Mr. Enemy; BAD BAD BAD!

ha ha ha! I
Have become a prototype
Anime Child!
Ha Ha Ha!
ICE CREAM!

Blow green film
bubble gum balloon;
float away, little dinosaurs,
float away!

# MIDWAY:

I go Kamikaze for the stranger
to my right. "I'll take the hit,
just shoot out the turrets."
I can feel the stranger nod
and feel happy to have
a capable wingman.

We are 7 years old and
already we've become grizzled veterans
of the top-down Pacific Theater.

I use the last of my dwindling
life reserves, my ticking red bar,
to summon a storm that stops time
while my wingman attacks his targets.
He quickly clears the screen but
the last bullet, fired moments ago,
slowly traveling ever down, guided
by an evil and fateful trajectory
catches my plane
just before the level ends.

"Man," my partner says, with
reverential sadness; "man..."

I nod, accepting my stupidity as
best I can while
he starts the next level
alone.

## PAC MAN:

The terror I experience
during my "tactical" flight
is very real, as real
as any nameless creeping
horror derived from any supernatural
stalking presence waiting
to seize me from the darkness
at my back while walking
down a black alleyway.

They are coming for me:
THEY ARE COMING FOR ME!
and I am
powerless
to stop them.

## DEFENDER:

I have no idea what I am doing
but I am doing it very fast.
Things are exploding into lines of
red and orange starbursts,
little pixel fireworks. Even though
I am sure that this means something bad,
like, maybe each little "PoP!"
is a human I should have tried to save,
I can't help but think that it's pretty.

Despite my cluelessness, I keep playing,
feeding quarters into the machine
just to watch the pretty colors, flying
across a blank vista of desolate
digital night wastelands, unaware
of any goal,
no objective but the ride itself.

# BOSS ENCOUNTERS:

my lasers and missiles
fill the screen with a
blinding fury of high-tech
death.

The boss, fifteen times
my size, flashes purple,
rockets peeling away
from launchers hidden
in his impractical skin.

I bob and weave, wending
my perilous way through
the deadly maze of ordinance
as if to say: Ha ha! You
suck!

He begins firing lasers
from his eyes, lasers
with the ability to track and think;
dodging becomes more difficult.
I dip to the bottom of the screen
dangerously close to the creature's claws
which click and twitch, psyching me
out. I know the pattern, boyo;
I've seen you before. You're not
fooling me, not this time.

I let go with another volley
as a planet in the background
disintegrates; my opponent
is now strawberry red. I foolishly
use all my bombs and

my elation
         turns
         to horror.

The creature roars,
stops time,
and explodes the universe.

         a moment of silence;
         everyone I know
         is now dead...
                  Good thing that I don't care.

The screen flashes white, strobing,
making it difficult to dodge
the firestorm my angry friend
is giving off as his shell disintegrates.

Hunks of planets whizz by
in the foreground. We are traveling
a million miles an hour against
a black surrealscape of streaking stars.
White on black, white, black, white, white
ROCK! ROCK! I veer off just in time.

Semi-circle storms of gatling gun fire
spray cross the screen like golden droplets;
My maneuverability has been reduced
to quarters of an inch; white knuckled
on the stick, "if it's not one thing..."
whistled from between my gritted teeth.

The firestorm takes on a hypnotic rhythm;
I can no longer tell whose bullets are whose;
I find this amusing for a moment,
imagining my spaceship destroyed,
my pilot shouting "Found one!"

I blast away the last bits of cockroach shell
covering my foe and reveal what I hope
is his final, true form: a giant tentacled
eyeball creature protruding from the lobes
of a green, gun-encrusted brain.
"Makes sense," I nod, sarcastically, and
dub him "Mr. Peepers"

The eyestalk begins focusing power from the void,
drawing in globules of multicolored energy;
I know that this is not good, and try to fire faster
each pull of the trigger launching an insanely huge
wave of multicolored death.

Mr. Peepers begins to vibrate; space
becomes whiter and whiter, spreading
from around his singular eye. He fires
a ridiculously huge beam of pink energy

which extends to the opposite end of the screen;
the burst goes on for twenty seconds as
I dodge asteroids and missiles and landmines
and anything else that moves.

Space becomes completely white.
Silence, again. Then
colors streak across the screen.
We are back where we started,
flying through the destroyed fleet.
Mr. Peepers leads me into the eviscerated
hulk of one of the cap ships.

Machinery breaks away from the walls
flying at me from all directions
as his scythe tentacles extend,
pulling him backwards down into the
husk of the destroyed flagship.
Giant chunks of metal rebound off the walls,
sparks flying, techno music plays, spurs us on;
lasers zinging everywhere, rockets spinning absurdly,
machine guns spraying like murderous fire hoses.

Just when it feels like I can't take it anymore,
when NO human being (no matter how god-like their
reflexes may be) could ever possibly hope to survive
the madness of navigating this ever changing
twisting maze of bullets and metal,
a great roar emits from Mr. Peepers.
He begins shaking, tentacle arms shearing off,
hurtling ever onward, down the core of the ship.

His brain explodes into a great ball of fire for reasons
that I cannot discern. His eyestalk floats, snake-like
above his burning brain, firing lasers in bright circular
patterns, but it's too late. I dodge them easily.
"Its curtains for you, Mr. Peepers!" I shout.

The eye's movements grow more frantic, as if trying
to detach itself from its own brain. If it weren't so totally
insane, it might strike me as kind of sad.

Another screech and the screen erupts into a great
jagged firestorm. Mr. Peepers' eye floats alone,
the lobes of his brain split apart and exploded like
flesh colored water balloons. He looks at me,
blinks, and then disintegrates into an explosive frenzy
that throws off great balls of multicolored light and energy.

The credits instantly begin to roll as screenshots
of earlier levels flash slowly and dimly on the monitor.
The music is terrible, the screenshots uninspiring:
I walk away feeling jipped.

# COCKTAIL MODE:


I dream of the days
when suit-clad businessmen
snuck away from their positions
in marketing and accounting
      (company men, all of them;
        fine fellows in good standing
        with the trustees and chairmen of high finance)
and rolled up their cuffs,
elbowing across a small screen set
into a table in a bar down the street,
a screwdriver or maybe a martini
at their side,
a smoking ashtray on an adjacent table
always within easy reach.

I picture the games of 9 A.M. Pacman
accompanied by a little hair of tha dog that bit ya
or lunch breaks shifting into high gear
over captured Galaga ships and burgers;
perhaps a secret, secretarial tryst derailed
by a particularly intense fling with the
Journey machine.

drinking,
    smoking,
        playing sweet hooky...

Everyone knew what was up, back then,
in those golden days before cell phones and email;
they understood the sweet satisfaction of an hour
utterly wasted

stealing away, pocket full of quarters,
delighted with the empty expense
of company time.

My only cocktail modes occur in my computer room,
brightly lit, clouds of smoke billowing
from the cigarette clenched in my teeth,
slurping on Mickey's Big Mouths with Chad.
We huddle around my keyboard and joystick
trying to beat Metal Slug 3 on M.A.M.E.;

it's not the same, but it does the job well enough;
I only wish I could have gotten my share
of those three years
when there was a lunch rush at the arcade.

## COUNTER STRIKE 0r:
## Black Elvis


Somewhere in Michigan there is a black Elvis plotting a comeback.
He reports that it's snowing mad outside
while premeditating his vengeance.
I picture him in a Christmas home,
lost deep on some suburban parkway,
whited out on all sides, a silhouette
of a pompadour lit up in a window by
blinking tree lights in the background.
There is a softshoe scrape as he sharpens his knife,
sitting there by the sill, and a faint "haw haw haw"
that hints of the smiles that are yet to come.

He is the Original, he says,
But, when it comes to Black Elvi, I imagine that Original
is a relative term.
a few close acquaintances of mine wander by and are amused;
they claim to be his children,
they covet the title of "Son Of The Original Black Elvis."
Who wouldn't? I do, and feel less than gifted
in the company of my quick witted compatriots.
But we're about to get our next shot now, Elvis
is presumably prepared,
and I check, just for the sake of whimsy,
the ledge outside the window to make sure
that not a frosty flake has fallen,
and that I am, indeed, myself.

## SKOOKIE SPRITE:


Ah, sweet whimsical deathbringer,
murderer of smurfs, cutter of the contest
    on your papier-mâché fly-wings
    you assault A site, rushing
    screaming dark rally cries: "YOU WILL GO UNTIL
    YOU DIE FROM IT!" or
    "I can't wait to eat their babies! Let's get em! HOORAY!"
    spraying mad bullets blindly, 5-sevens blazing;
pOp-Pop-pOP-POp jump-crouching through the doorway
a thousand snipers laying in waiting,
trigger fingers trembling,
scopes all a flutter, scanning;


    (while some choose to circumvent the firing squad,
    flanking them, or sliding up from behind,
    with flashing knives slicing air like mad conductor's batons,
    you appear right in front,
    juking, diving, mad; a thousand well-aimed bullets
    burn a cartoon outline around you);


as your laughter begins, so do the screams.
"oh my god"... a tremor of fear running down the spine
of the enemy team; they hear the shotgun's pump,
the distant deagle report; they see the casualty lists,
the tiny radar ticks going red, blinking out,
they feel the silence... they fear the railroad tracks;
they fear your promise of New Zealand:
    NEw zEEIANd; the railroad tracks, the spawning ground
    of the Skookie Sprites; you will return them
    there, take them all to that terrible crossing

and show them why children weep at your name;
WHIMSY! MIRTH! ATTACK! GOGOGO!...

Skookie of the many projects. Never had a malicious
thing to say; "I love you" screamed angrily after getting killed;
"We're going to be Super Friends... FOREVER!"
always inviting someone new to join your club, always
looking for something different and psychotic, some
secret resonating frequency within the game...

As a tactician, you were less than nothing;
one strategy belied your guileless plan,
GO!    running into the fray, blinded by flashbangs
and pummeled by grenades, often, you were
silenced. It didn't matter to you.
So long as there was death in the world (even your own)
you were delighted.

And, for every triumph, there were at least three failures;
never climbed the stats like you thought you would, the
CLQ always showing you as another obsessed but inefficient
killer (even though your moments were awesome). Once,
While playing as Counter Terrorist on the ledge in Dust 2,
you killed an entire team, alone,
with nothing but a pump and a dream;
they came at you from all sides over and over again,
barely enough time to reload the shells before
blowing another one back, screaming at the LAN:

"COME ON YOU MOTHERFUCKERS; JOIN THE
SUPAH FRIEND CLUB! I FUCKING DARE YOU!"

invoking Cagney and Jimmy Stewart beating back the deadly push;
"YOU'LL NEVER TAKE ME ALIVE, COPPERS!
NEVER! NOT WHILE I GOT THIS PUMP IN MY HANDS!
ONE OF US IS GOING TO JAIL AND IT'S NOT GOING TO BE ME!"

What a character; what
a psychotic identity.
    Such joy in your triumphs;
    Skookie Sprite has set us up the bomb...
    Skookie Sprite has gone crazy and is executing the hostages;
    Skookie Sprite is knifing a wall, jumping up and down
        saying "I'm in position" over and over again.
Skookie Sprite chuckles darkly and begins digging the graves;
and, finally, after the Skookie of the Spriteland has
been laid low by an MP5 round to the face,
he remarks calmly of it in chat saying
"Oh No! Brains in my balaclava? again!?
Skookie explodes into glitter and laughter"

You always had the radio menu up, and took great joy
at being able to issue one last command from the grave;
the raspy whisper crackles through the static
of the infinite ether(net);
"I'm In Position; Go Go Go!"

## LIVING ROOM BALLET:
## (a tragedy)


I get all my poetry in movement
From fighting games on the PS2;
But there, the technique is flawless
Each beautifully fluid motion
Frozen in perfect form, replicated
With the tap of controller buttons, at will.

intoxicating beauty, though,
in those puppet models, in their
fluid flips, holds, Drunken backwards
striking kickface streaks of limbs
cartwheeling round the centrifuge of
Their digital weightlessness,
their simulated gravity.

I can drink and smoke and shout and scream,
play while watching old episodes of MST3K,
or listening to Brahms or Tom Waits,
Can pause it all and piss when I please...
And,
            once they inject human souls
into my 3d fighters, souls
with the capacity to fail
in their execution,
to find disappointment in lapses of technique
well, fuck it;
the ballet will have nothing on me.
and the artifice will have no end.

# OREGON TRAIL:

Every Thanksgiving, the cousins would come up
from Yuma and Roll and
we would place their names on their tombstones
after they died of dysentery,
cholera
or other maladies of the trail.

Little Sarah, for instance, fell ill
after being driven for too long; no rest on this train,
kids, I would say... we gotta make time.
I want to be in St. Louis by breakfast.
As an eight year old, I was a sadistic task-master.

A Banker from Chicago, I pictured my character
as being an amalgam of every mean father
from every Disney film I had seen. Our pace
was always grueling,
our rations always meager
(this, despite our huge stockpiles of food),
and, after I learned about the Donner Party
in social studies,
our decisions unquestionably disastrous:

Let's ford the Columbia River, I would say,
a malicious twinkle striking my eye as I
surveyed with glee the impossibility
of such a task.
Let's stop and hunt for an hour or so (the kids
starving like Ethiopians in the back as
I grabbed my pith helmet and canteen; I would
smack their hands as they reached into the giant
bags of grain; "I said I'll go hunting... don't
spoil yourself!" I'd shout, before returning
with a squirrel and a sheepish smile
standing over yet another corpse.)

And there were many corpses:
I turned the trail into a death march.
Indeed, when we were younger, someone would,
inevitably, end up crying after they died;
ever the tyrannical diplomat, I would allow them
to write their own epitaphs to mark their places
along our trail of tears.

I was always thrilled when we passed another one
of our gravesites (which appeared with ever-increasing
frequency as spots were filled):
Here Lies Brent, Took ill With Dysentery and
        Just Couldn't Hack It.
Here Lies Margo, Died of Exhaustion, the Lazy Bitch.

The only joy in my party came when God Himself
finally decided my cruelty had to end;
there would be tremendous cheering
at the news of my demise, a great sense of liberty
would sweep through the wagon as they trucked away
from my tombstone
(Here Lies Seth: Bitten by a Snake. What a Dick".
"I hope you break an axle!" I would shout
after them; "then you'll be sorry you killed me!
I did it all for you! Don't ya see? It was all for you!!"

After our journey's end (or after there was
no one left to bury the last member of our party)
we would file up the stairs of the pit,
the young children of the house, relieved
to be delivered from the harsh trail to our true
destination:
sitting over turkey cut by grandpa
and shimmering canned cranberry, ah,
Thanksgiving Dinner.

# MANIFEST DESTINY:

It strikes me as strange
now in the early strains
of my adulthood, that
Never once did I think of our bold
Westward Ho! expansion
as being part of the greatest
marketing coup in the history
of the grand US of A;
Striking out with such confident steps
on unsteady and unsure terrain,
fording giant rivers, floating wagons,
eating oxen during the winter
and climbing huge peaks as if
this was what one just does,
as if it took no courage, just
belief, a conviction, a greater
idea of prosperity, out there
after the bad times, after
we get settled
after we kill all the buffalo
and break the backs of the Indians;
Where is this place? This
land of peace and plenty?
Just... over there... over the next hill
Just out of sight... a walk
a little going
that's all it takes,
just a little gumption.
come on. It'll be easy.
I promise.

# KAGE:

on a quest for paper towels
commissioned by my mother,
I search the musty shadows
of the giant garage, murk
and cobwebs clinging
to my shaking fingers.

My parents do not yet realize
that our warehouse-sized
car-receptacle is ruled
by a gang of phantom Ninjas
led by Raiden, god of thunder,
master of lightening. I learned of him
from "Big Trouble In Little China,"
and know that he is real.

I grab the rolls of Bounty
and flee, feeling the darkness
close in around me, hearing
the nimble mouse-tap footsteps
of Kage, Raiden's fearsome lieutenant,
on the wooden rafters high above me.

I return to the kitchen,
breathless
and excited;
although I get scared
when thinking of their deadly silence,
in truth
I love the Ninjas
and know that they would never
really harm me with their games.

I place my dusty package on the counter,
imagining that it is some powerful
magical relic, and that I am lucky
to have stolen it from the assassin's lair
and still return with my life intact.

# THE LONG NIGHT OF THE LAW:

as darkness descends upon the city
a lone criminal, now reformed,
pilots a military chopper against the skyline.

Tommy-boy has been converted. He now sees
the error of his ways, and wishes only
to pay his debt to society in the currency of corpses,
the only real coinage he understands.

So, the hunt for traffic offenders begins.

a sedan full of punk hoodlums that ran a red
a sports car that brodied through a stop sign
a jaywalking grandmother
and other, vile
criminal
scum
are sentenced, signed, fate-sealed
and delivered to their just rewards with
dumbfire hellfire rockets.

Tommy laughs and screams in vicious New York mob cackle
into the radio as the cops close to pursue him;
he wheels the chopper round,
tail rotor spinning free and easy through
the stratospheric mist, narrowly avoiding a
billboard; he brings the bird around and
unleashes a torrent of bright smoky white
that blows the pursuing VCPD heli into
an adjacent building.

a target blip goes up on his radar
and he banks South, towards the airport;

rogue baggage handlers have lost some luggage.
ALL must be punished. EVERYONE is
equal under the eyes of the law.
His rockets bear this out. Make it true.

II

By the time the feds show up to chase the black rotor blades
of death and doom that have been set loose upon the city,
Mr. T has become something of a dreaded scourge,
a mythological evil, a plague upon the land
swooping from a thousand feet to street level
raining a meteoric strike of smoky white rockets
straight down onto his targets.

Occasionally, the feds get out of their cars
and set up fire teams, trying impotently
to stop the madness of one man and one machine.
Tommy laughs, knowing their games; silly feds,
he says, this is my case. Back off! he
shreds them into bits of gore, their
ATF caps blowing on the wind drummed up
from his spinning blades.

that'll show them; trying to take ME off the case...

He checks the ammo gauges which always read "FULL"
and continues with his work.

III

It's three AM by the time the National Guard tanks
roll into town, mobilizing in armored columns
crossing the bridges of suburbia, setting up
anti-aircraft positions downtown, black smudges
in the shadows of buildings. Tommy
shakes his head; he knows they haven't got a chance.

He checks his intangibles;
Time: 0070
      (whatever the fuck that may mean; the counter
      resets itself at 79 minutes)
Kills: 1,000+
      (a fine evening's work already)
Money: well, he's pulling 50 mil per kill, so
      (minus the time it took to steal the cop outfit
      and get into the military base)
    he's up for the night.
He sighs, wipes his strained eyes, yawns
"sleepy" he says into the radio like a little kid
      (with a thousand angry cops and authoritarians listening in)
as he opens up on a tank.
Happy little Tommy issues a warning:
"Enemy armor: be advised, this is my town now."


IV


At a quarter to 4, his precious night wings
took some serious damage from a few punks
who didn't have the good sense to die in the
fiery wreck of their soon-to-explode car.
Rather, they bailed and stood by its torchlight
popping their shotguns and rifles up
at Tommy's 6; brave heroes trying to
stop the tyrant's nightmarish reign of cruelty
and madness. Their car exploded and killed them all
but the damage was done. Having no HUD
or health bar, T leans out his now open cockpit
and shakes his head at the black smoke pouring from
under the metal skin of his tail rotor.
This complicates things somewhat, he thinks,
(fifteen speeding cop cars crashing into each other below him)
but not by much.


he swings the chopper in the direction of his car lot,
heading West for Sunset.

Upon arrival, he brings the chopper down suddenly,
smashing the fucker into the ground as if it were
a tinker toy angrily discarded by a fierce and petty God.
He bails from the crippled metal frame and is only slightly
sad to see the crushed corpses of some of his gang members
smeared on the macadam beneath his broken steed.
Having no time to grieve (The Law never rests),
he hops the glass divider and descends down the driveway
to his seven garages. He grabs a civilian car from one
slams it into reverse
and resprays it in the adjacent paint and body shop... sirens
and tanks rumbling in the distance.
He hops out, leaving the engine running; checks the time;
15 seconds as a lawman left. He sprints
to another garage and hops in the paddy wagon.
Solves one problem; time 0070. Good.

The stars blink for a time and then blink out.
Silence. The purr of his chariot under the dash,
the crackle of the radio as two cops stake out a
speed trap; these are a few of his favorite things.
The rest of the world is silent.
He is no longer wanted.

He throws the immense wagon of doom into reverse
and drives past the hulking wreck of his chopper,
the wheels losing traction on the guts of his goons.
Have to get that cleaned up, he thinks; bad
for business...

He does not wait for an opening in traffic. Sirens
off, he makes one, barreling through the intersection, a
"FUCK YOU, BUDDY!" comes from a cut-off car.
Tommy slams on the breaks;
pauses. Deep breaths; I really should go back
and kill that fuckface... lewdness in a public place,
disrespecting an officer of the law, interfering
with police business; the offences are petty but
they still make him dizzy with anger. Sigh;

can't afford to attract attention. Fuck it,
he says, and slams the wagon back into gear, the first hints
of sunlight appearing on the coast,
a pulsing red and orange corona.

He drives through the airport underpasses,
navigating like a professional crack head,
careening off of walls, swerving only to avoid
pedestrians and fellow policemen.

He rolls into the military base at full dawn, waves
to Bob the gate guard who nods back. Tommy
smashes through the swizzle stick booth bar anyway;
he knows that it does not go up.

Some of the camo dudes are up early, drilling.
Tommy nods in approval; Rigor. Training. Order.
He loves these things now,
but still, there is an itch at his trigger finger
(well-repressed, but present). He wonders
how many he could kill before they took him out.
Not enough, that's for sure.

He hops out, climbs the steps, stands silhouetted
for a second against the waking dawn, stretches his
shoulders, checks the time, feeling good,
then breaks into a sprint that an Olympian would envy.
Past the confidence course, through the chainlink gate,
around the tents and
back into the safety of his airborne battleship.
Time reads 0070; kills
1500+ Cash: pulling half a billion per level now.

He calls no tower for clearance before taking off;
camo dudes scramble for cover under the wake of the blades.
Tommy smiles and waves to his new friends as he
ascends, the same radar blips from an hour ago
wreaking havoc on his conscience.

V

After two normal hours (equivalent to six 12 hour
periods in his world), Tommy looks around at his
ruined, rocket-scarred city; Fuck it, he says
and calls it quits. He's put his time in tonight,
he's done his job. He flies to his hideout
and bails, leaping from the chopper, high above
his skyscraper, falling like a leaf, arms flailing,
landing with a thud; he tucks into a roll that does nothing
to defray the impact.
High above him, the chopper crashes onto the roof of his
apartment building and explodes in a great ball
of compressed gasoline and ordinance.

He stands, brushes his uniform off. Looks at
the (once again) newly rising sun. Some
feds roll up and he tosses two grenades
under their 4wd SUVs before ducking into his hideout
to save his game, laughing all the way.

I smile at the message on the screen:
"YOUR TIME AS A LAW OFFICER IS OVER."

# FISTS OF FURY:

I'm killing an endless stream
of zombies with a double barreled
shotgun when Alex walks into my room.

He watches silently for a time,
whistling and chuckling occasionally
at a great escape, sidestep, or juke.

"The trick is to not let them get behind you
or to let them back you into a corner," I
say, as I separate two of their heads from
their bodies.

"what do you do when you run out of ammo?"
he asks.
I turn away from the screen to face him,
my fingers still working the controls.
I smile ghoulishly:

"punch."

# BONDAGE:

I always thought that I was addicted to games, but once we got speed they would never stop running on and on for moon up sundown long periods that were impossible to determine just the death the death and the death the scoreboard flashes up on the screen jumping like a demon startling me out of my wits when the fuck did we hit two hundred?

Colonial Trevlaine speaks with a southern accent praising his god for resurrecting him in the stacks and I am crazy hat man seven feet tall made for headshots dressed all in ridiculous white like the mad hatter top hat arent you coming to my tee party I scream hunting my three guests with a grenade launcher through the gloom and misery of prox mined basements.

Enough enough enough never enough never enough always another round in progress more lines on the way another gram another gram another gram headshot you fuck with the magnum; well I write the book of klob: "the name's Klob; James Klob" pass the tray pass the tray.

Meanwhile the socio political implications of my Sociology class are debated for weeks on spun weeks on spun end like a hydroplaning car as I struggle to stay ahead of (X) whose coming after me with all the guns and I just got the chop and the hallway is exploding all around me as he sprays the walls with suppressing fire making sure I don't get in a door and hide coming at him from the knees chop chop chop chop! I am gibbering squealing like a pig most undignified in the duel but funny as hell with (X) doing his baby voice, entreating me to surrender to my fate and I scream in hysterical return like a rat in a maze or Nhym no way out ya see, just the air ducts and its then that both I and (X) start screaming simultaneously "ITS MOVING DAY! MOVING DAY!!" and the hysterical carnival of laughter rises up and we do more pickup the paused controllers right where we left off "and when we last left our heroes…" I say giggling only to FUCK YOU because my screen goes red (X) suffused with the glass energy -the super fuel moves of Jet Li- and my perspective is tumbling to the floor like a head rolling off the guillotine.

The madness is so profound here, fecund the air wet and moist with the crystal the ammonia breath what is the total number of hours in seven days? I remember the sixth for it was the worst: something bad in the air not just the rank cloud of cigarette smoke that hung like a demon haze. (Y) and I are in the bathroom world debating. we went in at three in the morning and it's seven at night and we are stunned; the complexion of everything has changed and we are gibbering psychos my notebooks running on running on into elaborate calligraphy from my childhood chronicling this vast wasteland so we sit and go at it for a while, trying to summon the feeling of clean by murdering with pistols in the caves which I hate because you can never know that map as well as the next guy.

eventually, I stand, stretching, as the tray comes my way again, with the last of the third g and I look around after cutting and snorting grunting like a pig I chase the drip lean back with cigarette clenched in my teeth and begin to slowly moan "when Mosses was in Egypt land…" (Y) jumps in with me "Let My People Go…"

# THE LAY OF THE LAN:

I sit in jeans on cold concrete
screwdriver in teeth, a mad pirate of technology.
My booty, computer husks, surround me:
Gunmetal gray cases
Mini-towers, heatbricks, ancient, Japanese
servers with huge heatsinks installed above the CPU; curious.
I have one monitor. I scramble cross the floor,
dirty, filthy, insane; no sleep; have
to get this all up and running too soon.
I plug in NICs like a switchboard monkey
make connections, run CAT 9 cross the floor
stare into the guts of machine number 5;
shit, the graphics must be on-board
I scribble notes on a stained and dusty receipt:
1 motherboard, ATA, three slots - check the processor later.

We are building a monster, no, an army of monsters
and it is wonderful. They will be strong and fast
and will make us rich and proud; they will run
Counter-Strike and the people will come in, dazed
from The Strip, and, after three dollar hours,
will leave as broke as any casino goer.
The sun is coming up; I can see it dappling the concrete
through the dirty storefront windows.
we will be ready.

I will make us ready.

## SMASH TV:


The sun had just begun to come up
when Joe lost his mind, smoke pouring
from under the hood of his ancient
post-apocalyptic Honda;
"See! I FUCKING told you!" he
laughed and screamed, mirthful in his
madness, delighting in the carnage of his hopes.


standing in my driveway, the church across the street
alight in early reds, framed by a cloudline
that would burn away in several hours he said:
"Well, fuck it...
this place is a vortex; I fucking called it;
I said that something would happen; DIDN'T I
FUCKING TELL YOU something would happen!"
and then he let out a savage yell as he hurled his
keys into the rocks that were our lawn;


i stood there laughing for a moment, but
trailed off, lost in the magic of
that deep and secret twilight, the
sunrise of the damned
        (secretly glad; Joe would not
        be going to Texas any time soon;
        the summer, for the moment, was saved;
        ordinary routines would not be postponed)


after some time spent staring at the newly born shadows
extending slowly from the streetlight poles
pouring like navy colored ink across the pavement,

Joe shifted and sighed;
"fuck it", he said, and produced from the
open trunk of his car a bottle of So Co.
a fucking handle of it, a grip of booze,
bright amber, deep, prismatic in the
dying cool of the early hours.
"I was saving this for Dallas,
But might as well..."
I agreed, and we retired to the guest room
where we could smoke and talk without disturbing my parents.

at a loss for entertainment in this room,
this too clean place, this family equivalent of
the Holiday Inn, I scavenged in the closet
where my mother had stored my childhood toys,
looking for something to do; I think
it was there that I found the old Super Nintendo.
Drinking off a whole glass of So Co. on the rocks,
I held the gray box of the console up for Joe's approval;
he nodded, ragged.

I hooked the machine up to the old TV,
hunted for the controllers, and dug through games
while Joe recorded the travesty of his
attempted escape from Vegas into the
microphone of a Playschool tape player.

In my mind, now, it reminds me very much of Thompson,
but, imagine in the place of the giant reel to reel
recording unit he lugged with him, he paced
the hotel rooms of Vegas with a brightly colored
child's toy; a piece of audio equipment made
to play Raffi tapes and vinyl dubs of Read and Listen
Star Wars stories.

we had somehow secured the world's largest bags
of Starburst Fruit Candy ever made,
(two, actually; two separate bags of sweet flavor,
monstrous in their Super Size),
and had just begun eating them as if
they were real food when I found the only
game in that part of the house that was 2 player;
Super Smash TV.

I looked over at Joe, pacing, smoking,
throwing back his glass and popping Starbursts
like a junky on pills, ranting into the
yellow microphone of the recorder;
"Joe," I said, "we're in trouble," waving
the game cartridge at him from across the room.


II
there are some games that just scream:
I AM THE WORLD'S BIGGEST SEMIOTIC-SPAWNED
OVERDOSE OF THEORY MADE INTO A PACKAGEABLE
AND MARKETABLE EXPERIENCE: BEHOLD: MY SEVERE
IRONY, AND MARVEL! MARVEL AT HOW MUCH YOU ENJOY
EXISTING IN MY ABSURD THOUGHT PROBLEM.

Smash T.V. was just such a game.

the corpse-piles generated from the furious skirmishes
that occurred in all the other games in the history of the world
could never touch the amount of mighty-jack
kill-em all gun-em down, every damn one of them,
murder spree-spawned gat gat gat gat-ting that
went on in the universe of Smash TV.

Imagine:

You, lucky contestant, have been selected
to be locked in a room in which you
will be attacked by several hundred people per
minute (most of them armed with riot clubs, bats, etc.);
they streak like insects into the small square room,
screaming, frothing at the mouth, hungry
for your blood, a human wave,
a deadly swarm of green shirts moving towards you
and only you.
Your job: kill them all. Kill them
with whatever you have; a machine gun
a flamethrower, a bat, a bazooka,
a gatling gun; it doesn't matter;
someone is going to die, and (for your sake)
it's not going to be you.
from the outset, it is clear:
no one will walk away from this contest.

Meanwhile, all of this skull blowing action
is being broadcast live across America, where,
presumably, the bloated and psychotic populace
watches with glee, swilling beer and
munching TV dinners

I always liked to imagine my friends
cheering for me; what the
fuck would that feel like? what kind
of life would that be? "Kill them all,
Seth; come on, you can do it!" or
my math teacher, willing my trigger finger
to mow down an angry mob of faceless lunatics

all through the heroic carnage, the
absurdly happy and completely inoffensive
announcer screams things like
"BIG
MONEY!  BIG
PRIEYZES:
I LUUUUUUV  IT!"
after you cleared a room and picked up
the thousand or so VCRS and Stereos
that magically spawned as your reward
for your mythic slaughter of your enemies.

Occasionally, you'd come to an empty room
and the walls would be blown out by something
hideous: perhaps a huge torso sewn into a tank
tread, or maybe some kind of disgusting slime
thing, red balls that explode when you touch them,
or mini-tanks, or laser mines, or little
automatic guns that were really hard to kill,
hunting you in packs as you ran around the room,
trying to evade their merciless onslaught
of deadly bullets;

it was one of those rare games that was
shocking, horrific, funny, disturbing,
fun, difficult, rewarding, and existential;
existential in the sense that, when
one comes face to face with a thousand things
that want one thing and that thing is to
tear your arms out and eat you, quarter you,
flambé you, throw your genitalia in the air
in celebratory actions, barbarous and insane,

(all for the benefit of a live studio audience
and millions of viewers at home),
one can't help but stop and wonder what it must be like
to actually exist in such a universe;
contemplating the horrible possibilities of human cruelty,
the garish nightmare of the game show,
the sick greed, the stupid rewards, the pointless
slaughter of chance; the grinding lack of excitement.

By the time Joe and I got to the final boss,
we were drunk madmen, starburst juice
running in big sticky strings of multicolored
drool through our beards as we cackled insanely;
it became difficult to play because of the spasms
of laughter that rang through us like
church bells; the sun was up, the bottle was dead,
the starburst wrappers like autumn leaves in hawaii,
covering the floor of the room like snow and skulls,
like three hundred dead butterflies killed
by bullet hail and lightening guns;
the last room in the game was a very special place;
it was made of red carpet instead of cold concrete
or blank steel; I bet it smelled good in that room;
less corpses; few got there.

The last room was very quiet. Kind of a waiting space;
a place of shuffled feet and "so, humm"s,
fingers in belt loops while waiting for the elevator
or the intercom or

the announcer, in person, appearing.

III

a lot of people say that, when they see someone
from TV in person, that they looked
a lot different in real life.
Taller, shorter; bad skin, good skin:
terrible hair, etc.
Well, nowhere was this more true than in The Announcer.

He was dressed in his usual sequined jacket, (red),
his big smile beaming, full of love,
with teeth that sparkled like sanatorium stairs;
Dentyne brightness; blue eyes, tanned skin,
coiffed hair; everything was in place when we met him.
He looked just like he did on TV.

Except that he was several stories tall,
had no legs (tank treads; a real talking
head; no pants under the desk, newscaster
gone mad; media puppet made into a slave
god of Rupert Murdoch's death factory),
and his arms (come ta think of it, Joe,
we never did see his arms; oh MY GOD!)
ended in rocket launchers that spewed bullets,
bodies (yeah, interesting, eh?), drone guns,
tank people, flames; anything that could kill many
and very quickly.

We howled and attacked him like jackals,
screaming, yipping, hopping, being thrown
across the room, unloading arsenals into his gut,
but he just kept laughing, and the whole thing
was so insane at this point, we could no longer take it,
we began screaming, gibbering insane half-thoughts

of total madness, repeating, mimicking the
monster we were trying to do in; what tremendous fun
it was, fighting media-evil born on tank treads;
what sick and crazy fun.

And, after he was dead, we could scarcely move
from all the furious laughter, the bright and shining
psycho mirth of the truly shattered, the living;
the really living.

And we had won.

## HAVEN'T PLAYED IN YEARS:

I play the old games that I mastered
as a child,
and find a tightness rising in my chest, an
unaccountable anxiety at every move,
every twitch
of the stick
or tap
of a button.

I wonder why, for a moment, but
the answer comes to me; floats up
from the center of my mind.

I am now both players. I am
competing against the memory
of myself; each time
I fire up MAME, I
compete with the little me
that still lives inside. He says shit to me,

backhanded advice:

No! Not like that! Don't you know ANYTHING?

JUMP! Now shoot. USE YOUR MISSILE!
See; I told you. Let me! Let me!

He screams, jumping up and down.

Let ME do it! Let me play!

Like any other child,
I find his presence charming, depressing,
and irritating.

It's ok though; I kick his ass on the PS2.

# MY AFTERLIFE:

I am playing Pitfall.
Blocky green and yellow on
a TV in a dark room just before
Sunset, smooth,
with the smell of the rubber
and the click of the fat controller
buttons.

I think I might go out later,
maybe with my Dad to play a dollar worth
at Nickelodeon
(five cent games!)
But right now I am ok; I think about it,
though, as I try to escape the scorpion.

II:

I chuckle, seeing Kurt Weil playing volleyball
with street kids out in front of
Charleston Heights.
Just down the street, Fatha Hines
and Louis are working through Weatherbird Rag
by the old bowling alley.
Heard rumors that they're going to build a casino there;
one of these days.     But right now
the afternoon is like the first silence
after the end of a song.

III:

I do not drink in this world;
Everything fuzzy and interminable
Fresh and thrown together, curbstones
in a crazy small town.
Bamboo swordfights at the real world,
in the concrete cage, under chain link sky
with blasted smudge sand-people desert all around,
glowing in the dusk.

I think of these things as I pass the controller
to Tom Waits and remain unmoving for eternity,
in the Pit with its huge bay window
Feebly blocking the sun with broken blinds,
razors of sullen gold breaking patches of glare on the TV,
Nine years old and finally home.

CONTINUE?
10

# APPENDICES

"We lived many lives in those whirling campaigns, never sparing ourselves any good or evil; yet when we had achieved, and the new world dawned, the old men came out again, and took from us our victory and remade it in the likeness of the former world they knew. Youth could win, but had not learned to keep, and was pitiably weak against age. We stammered that we had worked for a new heaven and a new earth, and they thanked us kindly, and made their peace. When we are their age, no doubt we shall serve our children so."
- T. E. Lawrence

"Every hero becomes at last a bore." - Ralph Waldo Emerson

# Appendix A:
# IMMORTALS
(Presented with an absolute disregard for ordered thought)

**Fallout2** (the greatest game ever made)
**Metal Gear Solid**
**Castlevania: Symphony of The Night**
**Excitebike**
**Dragon's Lair** (and **II: The Time Warp**)
**Joust** and **Joust 2**
**Pitfall**
**Discs of Tron** – Not the arcade machine that had the light cycles game from the movie along with several other depictions of other games from the film; Discs of Tron was a separate arcade machine that only had this game on it.
**Q*Bert** - A perfect example of a game that made absolutely no sense.
**Counter-Strike**
**Spelunker**
**Metroid** (and **Super Metroid** for the Super Nintendo)
**All three Super Star Wars** games for the Super Nintendo
**STAR WARS** - The arcade games based on the first and third movies; Atari did make a game based on the 2nd film, but I never really liked it that much.
**Magician Lord** - The first Neo Geo game (SNK) that I played in the arcade. You play as a blue wizard (no relation to the title of this book) who, coincidentally, is always about to die. I remember it as being a great sidescroller with awesome graphics and above average gameplay.
**Bionic Commando**
**Legend of Kage**
**Sam and Max Hit The Road**
**ZORK I** and **II** - Especially **II**; its puzzles were more logical.
**Bushido Blade I** (but not **II**)
**R-Type**
**Dig-Dug** (and **II**)
**Galaxian**
**Choplifter**

**COMMANDO**

*Shinobi 2 & 3*

**SHADOW RUN**

*System Shock*

*Ikari Warriors*

*50 Cal. Fifty Caliber* - A total rip off of Ikari Warriors with better graphics, more blood, and more varied gameplay. The console port of this game to the Genesis really sucked, though, and the game was really only good when it could still be played in the arcades.

*Guerilla Warriors* - Another total rip off of Ikari Warriors with better graphics and more varied gameplay. Why everyone looks like Che Guevara is a mystery to me.

**Syndicate**

**Donkey Kong**

**Indiana Jones and The Temple of Doom** (arcade)

**UNREAL TOURNAMENT**

*Doom* - Ya know, the most revolutionary game in computer history...

**Quake**

*Tekken 2* & *3*

*Soul Calibur* - Poor Voldo; although I did write a poem for him, I felt that it was way too fan-boyish. See the website as I may post it there.

*Bump'N'Jump* - Nothing made more sense to me than jumping over cars with (you guessed it) a car. This was (and still is) an extremely fun game to play (despite the insanity of its premise).

*F-Zero* and its second incarnation on the N64

*Dark Forces* and *JEDI KNIGHT: DARK FORCES II*

*Dr. Chaos* – This is, bar-none, hands-down, the worst video game ever made. I don't care what anyone has to say; this title for the NES was SO intolerably bad that I could not believe the developers didn't go into exile after its release. Incorporating every element of a bad game (terrible control, bad graphics, impossibly poor level design, etc. etc.), Dr. Chaos is a testament (and lasting reminder) as to how unutterably wrong the development process can go. I still have my cartridge only because I don't want to waste my time smashing it.

**ARKANOID: Revenge of DOH** - Useless fact about this game: Did you know that the paddle was called the "vaus"? Nope? Well, now you know; go impress your friends.

**XEVIOUS** - MAME really brought this game back to me. This game was a lot of fun because you could attack ground targets while simultaneously shooting airborne discs and other abstract shapes meant to represent ships of some sort. I guarantee that you have played this game; you just have to see it once and it all comes flooding back like some sort of drunken dream.

**Rush'N'Attack** - Not really one of the greatest games ever made, but it's impossible to omit from any list of truly memorable arcade titles. This game was included in the first "Player's Choice" Nintendo arcade cabinets from the Eighties. In it, you play the part of a one-man answer to the Commie-pinko-bastard Soviet invasion of America. It's interesting to consider the roles video games *didn't* play in terms of propaganda; I didn't know a single person who cared about the political message of this video game (but, in retrospect, the fuel for semiotic analysis is dizzying).

**Cloak and Dagger** - Notable for being the 2nd game I played that got made into a movie that actually featured the game in the film. The first, of course, was Tron. Jack Flack, baby; Jack Flack.

**Duke Nukem** - NOT the sidescrolling shareware platformers put out by Apogee in the early 90's, but the first 3D incarnation of this slick-talking hyperbolic action hero.

**Tomb Raider** - As much as I hate to say it (I never really liked these games), I can't bring myself to omit Lara Croft (superstar of stage and screen) from this list. Bah! As an early reviewer of one of the sequels put it, "I shudder at the thought of the programming hours spent trying to make her ponytail move 'just so.'"

**Noctropolis** - Very few people remember this game, but it remains one of my favorites. It was released for the PC just after programmers had been able to integrate full motion video into "traditional" game interfaces. The artwork in this game was absolutely, drop-dead stunning. Also noteworthy for containing the first scene of frontal nudity I can recall in a video game.

**Space Harrier** - I refuse to believe that the programmers of this game were not under the influence of some serious psychopharmacopic substances.

**Afterburner**

**NARC** - Ya know; for kids!

**Crystal Castles**

**Wizards and Warriors** - The side scrolling platformer for the NES which was, coincidentally, the second game I played that used the opening of the Unfinished Symphony as its title music.

**Thunder Castle** - I have vague recollections of this old Intellivision title being great fun to play, however, it's listed here solely because it was the first game I remember that used the music from Schubert's Unfinished Symphony.

**Prince of Persia**

**Karateka**

**Weird Dreams** (for the old IBM 386)

**Double Dragon** - Weird, but I never enjoyed playing this game. That having been said, my lack of enjoyment never prevented me from playing it.

**MAJOR HAVOC** - It only took me eighteen years and a hundred and fifty man hours to find the name of this game, one of my favorites from my childhood. See the website for detailed ravings about how much I love this game.

**Todd's Adventure In Slime World** (for the Lynx)

**720** (a.k.a. **SKATE OR DIE**)

**Moon Patrol**

**ASSAULT** - Atari's seminal (ok, so it came out it in 1988; sue me, it was seminal to me), top-down, "space tank" game. I never truly *enjoyed* playing this game, but I did play it all the time. Also remarkable for its capricious use of nuclear weapons and multi-leveled game maps.

**Goonies** (a.k.a. **"Vs. Goonies"** - why? We may never know.)

**Gauntlet** and **Gauntlet II**

**Duck Hunt**

**Sunset Riders** - (Konami, 1991) The bloodiest cowboy game ever made, this was unimaginably fun to play. With support for four players, good graphics, excellent gameplay, and more slaughter, booze, and frontier-dance-hall floozies than you could shake a stick at, this game remains one of my all time favorites from the arcade.

**Castlevania II** - The one in which you could be caught in the wilderness after nightfall, or in a city filled with zombies after the wolf howled...

**Tetris Puzzle** - Help save the suicidal Dr. Tetris from being entombed under an endless series of falling bricks.

**Puzzle Fighter** - Jeez.

**Xenophobia** - What a weird fucking game this was.

**HOOPS**

**Marble Madness**

**Paperboy**

**DRIVER** - Forgetting the regrettable fact that your character's name is "Dick Tanner," this PS1 title is my favorite car game ever (**Gran Turismo** is a close second).

**Strider** - I still remember the Bellog Air Ship and the anti-grav ending. What a great game.

**KARNOV** - Did you know that his real name was Jinborov Karnovski?

**Contra III: The Alien Wars** - The first game in the franchise for the Super Nintendo. This was my favorite 2-player sidescrolling shooter from those days. Magnificently cool.

**Blaster Master**

**Kung Fu**

**1943: Battle for Midway** (and the rest of the series)

**XENOS** - STRANGER: BEWARE! This was THE first TBAG (Text Based Adventure Game) that I played with my mom. Ichor, man; it's all about the green ichor.

**Faxanadu**

**Fester's Quest** (bizarre fucking game)

**Burger Time!**

**Gravitar** - So old! So totally forgotten!

**Hard Drivin'** - One of the few games from the eighties to live up to its title, this game was damn near impossible to master. Most will remember it for its inclusion of some really "Goddammnit-that-would-be-cool-if-I-could-just-do-it!" stunts, like the ability to drive your car through a vertical loop. This was also the first game to use 3D rendering.

**Gladiator** - Not the game where you fight in the sewers (**TROJAN**), but the arcade melee fighting game from the mid to late eighties in which armor would be knocked off of those who got hit.

**Tai Pan**

**Ghost** - The first sidescrolling rail FPS... for the old PC... wow. I think that this was the first game I ever played at home...

**Splatterhouse** - Listed here solely because it was the game that launched the video game violence debate in the late Eighties through the Nineties.

**Night Trap** - Listed here solely because it was the game that brought the video game violence debate back into the arena of national discourse due to its inclusion of FMV bikini girls getting off-ed by cheesy, B-flick caliber flunkies dressed in cheap black ogre costumes (er, "auger" costumes... yeah, whatever).

**Altered Beast**

**Time Traveler** - Proves, once and for all, that great graphics alone a good game does not make... This was a game that worked inside a special cabinet that actually generated three dimensional, free standing holograms on a table-top surface roughly the size of a dinner plate. Spectacular to behold in any era (the visuals were great back then, and would be great today), but the game itself was just awful.

**Jackal**

**Journey** - This game was based around the band of the same name and featured black and white images of the member's faces stuck onto stick figured bodies. I was unfamiliar with the band when this game came out (hell, I was three years old), and was both fascinated and disturbed by the psychotic visuals and utterly insane gameplay.

**BreakThru** - Man, I loved this game. You are a weaponized armored car (with the ability to jump, of course) cruising at top speed through devastated metropolitan areas (the vibe of the game was pseudo-post apocalyptic). This was a great game.

**Swashbuckler** - The pirate fighting game for the old Apple IIe

**Lemmings**

**The Simpsons: Bart's Nightmare**

**SINISTAR**

**Asteroids**

**Spectre**

**Bad Dudes Vs. Dragon Ninja** - Terrorist punks have kidnapped President Reagan. Are you bad enough to save the leader of the free world from the nefarious "Dragon Ninja"? I'm actually more ashamed of having played this game than I am about having played PONG. Also notable for featuring everyone's favorite huge, sweaty-breasted, fire-breathing Russian, KARNOV as an end-of-level boss.

**Irritating Maze** - Notable only for its severely irritating inclusion of an electro-shock joystick and pressurized air jets directed at your eyes.

**Alien Crush** - An amazingly bizarre and cartoony game that saw (from what I can tell) extremely widespread distribution in the Eighties. If you saw a screenshot of this game, you would instantly remember it.

**Mech Warrior**

**Crazy Taxi**

**APB**

**RASTAN** - See the website for a poem about this game.

**Black Tiger**

**Rainbow Six** - Most of the franchise. I played the hell out of these games during the late 90's; I particularly enjoyed moments when I would forget who I assigned the Go-Codes to. Red Group: GO! Oh, shit... shit shit shit... Suddenly, everyone is dead and the Tangoes have won. Great Game.

**Speed Rumbler** - I liked this game a lot just because you could get out of the frigging car if it was going to explode. At the time, I felt that this was a brilliant innovation in terms of realism.

**King's Quest** - They made so many of these games that I can't really recall which ones I enjoyed playing.

**Space Quest:** The Entire Franchise

...and several others that escape my memory

# Appendix B:
# What Happens When Linux Programmers Name Their Own Creations:

The following are all real games currently under development for the Linux operating system. They are (for the most part) the work of amateur programmers and hackers. Such people should NOT BE ALLOWED to name their games.... (* indicates a personal favorite)

Abe's Amazing Adventure
*Afternoon Stalker
Astro Battle
*Burger Space
CosmoSmash
Crazy Hendehoh
Deathchase 3D
*Evil Bricks
Falsoid
Gnome Attacks
GTK-Manix
*Infernal Contractor II
Kamikaze
*Mutant Storm
OQix
Pachie El Marciano
*Polyroids
Rock Dodgers
*Supercow!
Tadpoles
Taxipilot
Teutron
TickleTankle
*Tompong
Trackballs
XBill
Yanoid (Yet Another Arkanoid Breakout Clone)
Thrust

# Appendix C:
# An Account of Grue Hunting In The Great Underground Empire:

once I flipped out; the maze
was impossible; text text text text
fuck! my
lantern fizzled, died... no more fuel...
great.
"You have moved into a dark place.
      It is pitch black. You are likely to be eaten by a grue."

In eleven moves I was dead:

**?)** What is a grue?
**-)** The Grue is a sinister, lurking presence in the dark places of the earth. Its favorite diet is adventurers, but its insatiable appetite is tempered by its fear of light. No grue has ever been seen by the light of day, and few have survived its fearsome jaws to tell the tale.
**?)** Look.
**-)** It is pitch black. You are likely to be eaten by a grue.
**?)** Where is the grue?
**-)** There is no grue here, but I'm sure there is at least one lurking in the darkness nearby. I wouldn't let my light out if I were you!
**?)** Kill grue with hands
**-)** I've known some strange people, but fighting a lurking grue?
**?)** Eat the grue.
**-)** I don't think that the lurking grue would agree with you.
**?)** Touch grue.
**-)** Fiddling with the lurking grue doesn't seem to work.
**?)** Talk to grue

**-)** You can't talk to the lurking grue.

**?)** Kill

**-)** What do you want to kill?

**?)** Me.

**-)** What do you want to kill the me with?

**?)** Myself

**-)** You don't have the you.

**?)** Take grue.

**-)** An interesting idea.

OH NO! You have walked into the slavering fangs of a lurking grue.

You Have Died.

# Appendix D:
# List of References Contained In The Poems
# (And Other Points of Interest):

Despite the fact that I've always felt a poem requiring annotation is a poem that is worthy neither of reading nor writing, I've included the following pages of notes for two reasons. The first is to provide people who might not have played some of the video games mentioned in this book with a brief description of what is going on. The second is to share some of my otherwise useless remembrances of video game-oriented minutiae with those who remember the games in this book. I've done my best to ensure that all of the information presented in here is as accurate as possible.

The title of this book comes from "Gauntlet II", the sequel to the first "real" four-player game to appear in the arcades.

## MARIO:
Lines 8-17: Super Mario World (Super NES); Yoshi was a
    vaguely horse-like creature crossed with a turtle. Mario
    could ride this creature and, being mounted cavalry,
    could sustain another hit before dying or being reduced
    to his pitiful, mortal form. Yoshi was genetically gifted
    in that, after being incited to do so by a firm punch to
    the rear of the cranium, it would extend its tongue, a
    long, sticky, rather amphibious looking thing, which
    could attach to an enemy, pulling it into Yoshi's gaping
    maw.
Lines 20-21: At the end of each level in the original Super
    Mario Brothers, Mario would enter the main gate of a
    small, outpost-sized castle and a new flag (bearing a
    star, if memory serves) would go up the flag pole. In
    retrospect, the game really does make it seem like
    Mario is mounting a campaign against the feudal lands
    of King Koopah. Ostensibly, such military endeavors
    were justified as being necessary in order to save the
    kidnapped Princess Toadstool who was (from what I
    can remember) a member of the old ruling party of the
    kingdom. It should be noted, however, that these
    somewhat dark and pessimistic observations on the

geo-political implications of Mario's rise to power are being made by an adult looking back on the game, and do not accurately reflect my feelings during the relative innocence of my youth.

Lines 23-34: "Super Mario Brothers" for the original NES accounts for the single largest portion of Nintendo's sales (they've sold over a billion game cartridges during the life of their company). Out of this impressive tally of games sold, Super Mario Brothers accounts for a nearly unimaginable 40 million sold worldwide. And that's not including other games in the Mario franchise like Donkey Kong, Super Mario 2, or any of the other games. You and me, kid, millions!

## THINGS I'VE LEARNED:

Lines 4-5: "They trip trip wires/pick up grenades but can't find the pin..." The trip wire reference can be directly attributed to "Platoon", the game based off the movie for the NES.

Lines 7-9: Nearly a direct reference to "Ninja Gaiden", a game in which the player is somehow inexplicably capable of climbing on walls and ceilings (in theory, by using some piece of particularly clever ninja equipment that was never really explained). This was particularly fun to do; having the ability to scale sheer walls is inherently cool (see "Shinobi" if you doubt it). What was even cooler, though, was doing a backflip off the wall you were climbing and re-catching the wall as close as possible to the place where you jumped off, totally defying gravity for absolutely no reason. We practiced this a great deal, and anyone who remembers the game will recall what fun it was to demonstrate this maneuver to a spectating friend (especially for the first time; gamers love being able to find something new and undiscovered in a game that everyone else has already played).

Unfortunately, I was guilty of milking this particular gag by trying to perform it *all the time* (especially under circumstances that were somewhat less than ideal - i.e. while being attacked by other ninjas, during boss encounters, etc.), and (very often) would fail to return to the wall before hitting the bottomless pit that the bottom edge of the screen had become. Ah, the glory days of the platformer!

Lines 10&11: "they die at the hands of the Evil One direct..."
In retrospect, I find it extremely harrowing how often
any given character would die at the hands of their
arch enemy in a relatively fair fight. I say "relatively"
because bosses were almost always more powerful
than the hero who opposed them (the single most
fundamental principle of arcade games is to make
them just hard enough so that the kids will have to
spend more while still having fun dying). Bosses would
often appear in multiple layers of armor and with
special guns, and were always really hard to kill.

Still, I find it very depressing that I never cared about
the fact that my character lost and had (in essence)
utterly failed in the only quest that mattered to him or
her. We're talking about fairly epic things here, like
saving the world from some tremendous archetypal
evil, or avenging the deaths of loved one's, and, more
often than not, the hero (through want of the player's
ability) would simply lose. As a kid, I got used to this
lesson very quickly, and I suppose I carry it with me to
this day.

### THINGS I"VE EXPERIENCED:

Lines 1-3: Hitman II, Silent Assassin

Lines 4-9: P.O.W. (Prisoners of War)

Lines 10-11: River City Ransom

Lines 12-17: Metal Gear Solid

Lines 18-21: I can't remember the name of this game.

Lines 22-23: Fictitious; there is no game behind this
description.

Line 24: Nabunaga's Ambition

Pg 8: Lines 37-44: Mechwarrior ("Ambient temperature is
negative five hundred degrees Celsius; global mean
time is...")

Lines 45-50: WWII Fighters (my favorite flight sim of all time)

Lines 51-56: aggregate of X-Wing series, Privateer, Wing
Commander, etc.

Lines 57-59: (deep breath): Spelunker, Shinobi, Mega Man,
Doom, Quake, Goonies, Contra, Castlevania, Zelda II,
etc., etc., etc.

Lines 60-62: This is untrue, as is the depiction of the black
night in the Joust poem; after researching my

memories of the game, I realized that I had been thinking of the dreaded Pterodactyl, a creature that it is rumored you are able to kill...

Lines 63-65: Blue Thunder

Lines 66-70: Doom and Quake et all

Lines 71-74: Aggregate of Sniper Wolf from Metal Gear Solid and another game whose title I can't remember, possibly Golgo13

Lines 75-93: this deserves some explanation:

In Fallout2, the player takes on the role of "The Chosen," a member of a small village in the Southern California desert some fifty years after nuclear war. You are sent out of the village after passing the temple of trials in order to find the holy G.E.C.K. (Garden of Eden Creation Kit, a piece of standard issue equipment to the many thousands of people who took shelter in gigantic fallout vaults before the war.) In any case, the game had the most beautiful introductory cinema, presented like a 1950's instructional video about how to rebuild the world after nuclear holocaust. It was all set to Louis Armstrong singing "A Kiss To Build A Dream On", and still remains one of my most treasured memories of video games.

The actual reference itself refers to the caretaker of the vaults in Vault City (a location you discover late in the game). If you stand and watch this character, a speech bubble appears above his head and he sings a song that has taken me over seven years to find the sheet music for. The name of the song is "Maybe," and is not the famous one written by George and Ira Gershwin, rather, it is by a totally forgotten Broadway songwriting duo named Alden and Flynn. The words are as follows: "Maybe/ You'll think of me/When you are old and gray/Though Hans is the one who is/waiting for you/he'll prove untrue/I'll kill that cat, and/then what will you do?/ Maybe/you'll sit and sigh/Wishing that I/were near/and maybe you'll ask me/to come back again/and maybe/I'll say maybe." It is also worth noting that I knew this song before I played the game, and that, to this day, I still only have a single recording of it being sung (Doc Cheatham and Nic Payton; "How Deep Is The Ocean"). It is the most obscure Dixie Tune that I know of, and for it to appear in this awesome role-playing game broke my heart.

NOTE: Maybe wasn't written in the 20's. It was penned in 1932, and the lyrics presented above are not the original words.

Lines 101-102: Final Fantasy (insert sequel number here)

Lines 102-106: WWII Fighters; "Flack's opening up" is something you hear your wingmen say all the time, usually said very quietly over the radio, only to be followed by the screams of your wingmen dying.

Line 113: "This one's for you, Gerri..." This is also from WWII Fighters, but is from the intro cinema in which The Battle of the Bulge is depicted. The cinema is striking, set to the pulsing rhythm of "Sing Sing Sing." An allied fighter breaks from his wing and goes after a German bomber and delivers this line at the climactic conclusion just before the title screen comes up.

## *BUSHIDO BLADE:*

All the characters in this game were experts at a certain weapon. There was, incongruously, an Irish swordsman in this Japanese Dojo. He was my favorite character, and his ending was particularly sad. In fact, I am nearly certain that I mixed the endings of both the Dojo master and the Irish guy together in these two poems; they both killed themselves at the end of the game, but I think the dojo master actually fell on his own sword or committed Seppuku with a katana... the Irish guy had the dagger.

Line 6: The Russian chick was my second favorite character. Very much like the Irish guy, each one of her three stances (high, medium, and low) was so elegant that the pose itself was a stunning work of art.

Line 40: "... master blocking" If there was a single fault in this game it was that, after you learned all of your opponent's moves, tapping a single button would allow you to completely block and deflect any attack. The timing was pretty difficult to get down, but once you had it mastered, you were ridiculously powerful.

*General Note:* Unlike many of the other descriptions of gameplay in this book, most of which are meant to dramatize or more fully realize the actions depicted in the games (*Joust, Things I've Experienced,* etc.), everything in this poem occurred in the actual gameplay. You could throw sand in your opponent's face, cripple them, and could even honorably surrender in the event that you felt that you could not continue the battle (if you lose one of your arms and both your legs it becomes very difficult to win). Surrendering meant crossing your legs and presenting the back of your neck with your weapon held at your side. I got chills every time I saw this happen because it only ensured an honorable death; the opponent had to kill a surrendering enemy.

## CRAZY TAXI:
Line 13: A single round of Crazy Taxi could take as long as forty minutes of non-stop action. It became grueling and the perpetual rush often made you crazy.
Line 21: "Corporate Sponsorships..." Harley Davidson, Pizza Hut, and Levi's Jeans were all on board during this game's development phase and had their products featured in the game as stores that you would take your passengers to.

## KID ICARUS:
The depiction of the end of this game is completely accurate in my memory. The game threw a totally impossible maze at the player which could be traversed vertically and horizontally. It seemed hellish to me at the time; huge and deadly, with more wrong turns than I can remember.

## PAPERBOY:
Lines 3&4: "blondes in the black Dusenburgs..." At the end of every level of this game, the Paperboy must cross an increasingly busy street filled with these cars. As the player advances to the higher levels, the cars are more numerous and go faster and faster. The street also gets wider and becomes more difficult to cross. By the fifth level, it's damn near impossible to make it past these chicks without getting killed. The insane thing was that Paperboy could never stop; it would make the game too easy. Thus, he would always have to ride out into this vehicular firing squad.

## SINISTAR:
I failed to incorporate several things from the game in this poem, the biggest one being another line that Sinistar used to taunt the player with; "RUN, COWARD! RUN!" Utterly horrifying considering that there really wasn't any way to escape him at this point unless you had Sini-Bombs.

## 3D:
Line 17: Linux programmers will easily recognize this. /Dev/Null is,

essentially, a black hole for useless data. Anything that's "piped" (piping is the process of shunting data returned from a program into another program or file) to /Dev/Null is instantly erased.

### QUAKE: General Note:

Some of the best Mods I remember that were made for this game included:

The Grappling Hook: This was revolutionary at the time.

Ultra Gib: "Gibs" are the graphical display of a body after it has been reduced to its component parts by some explosive weapon. This mod made "gibbage" a super spectacle of flying gore.

Quake Rally: Described by some members of the mod community as the most breathtaking technical achievement of its time, this mod transformed the Quake engine into a fully realized car combat game with support for up to six players playing simultaneously. In my opinion, it was this modification (which took a little under a year for The Impact Team to finish) that opened everyone's eyes to what could be done with these game engines.

There were literally HUNDREDS of weapon modifications, all of which I have forgotten. In their day, they were awesome, but, after having downloaded custom weapons for many other games over the intervening years, I can no longer recall any of them specifically.

Line 12: An SDK (Software Development Kit) is a set of programming tools distributed to the general gaming public by the company that created the game. An SDK (amongst other things) allows hackers to really get at the guts of the game's engine (the system that the game sets up on a computer that effectively puts the game world together at run-time), enabling them to change the fundamental design and mechanics of the game. The release of SDK's has forever altered the way people play video games and, in a sense, has completely revolutionized modern computing as we know it. With a little time and patience (ok, a LOT of time and a LOT of patience), an amateur programmer can create almost anything and distribute it over the internet to other people who own the game. Such MODS and total conversion packages have played an as yet untold role in the development and proliferation of the internet itself, shaping what it could be used for and (in the early days) pushing the technical envelope further and further.

Line 16: The single most powerful asset the internet has and can provide is documentation of itself and of the programs that the computers which access the internet use. This facilitates the viral-like spread of knowledge that enables the internet to grow and change, and fosters a genetic cornucopia of influences, ideas, and perspectives in its development. While dry, technical programming of networks is a difficult thing to sell to the general public, the sheer fun of games like Quake spawned vibrant developer communities of kids and adults, all trying to understand how things worked so they could change it to reflect their desires. This, in turn, gave rise to in-depth level development guides and walk-throughs (which, in turn, got many people into programming and game design). Because of all of this, a novice can learn to make any dream they have into a living, breathing reality. That's the real miracle of the modern information age, and video games have played the biggest role in delivering these ideas to the laymen who have grown up along with these technological advancements.

**HALF-LIFE:**

"alien weapon that fired homing bugs..." This is inaccurate; there was no "gun" involved in the homing bugs that I was thinking of (the ones with the waterbug shell). Those homing bugs were "fired" by letting them walk off the palm of your hand and onto the floor, where they would proceed in a straight line until they hit either a wall or an enemy (often, after hitting a wall, they would turn around and kill you instead of your intended target... creepy). None of this is to be confused with the actual homing-bug-firing gun (another piece of alien technology from the game).

"the other weapons jammed..." but only in my imagination; this never happened in the game itself.

"The Man In The Blue Suit" Shortly before sending this manuscript out, I spent two days playing Half Life because I had to know what happened. I can now smugly report that the end of this game is... well, I'll let you beat it yourself; it's worth fighting for. No regrets, Freeman; no regrets. MUHAHAHA!

## MEGA MAN HAIKUS:

**General Note:** A Haiku is a Japanese poetic form using three non-rhyming lines composed of a set number of syllables (5-7-5 respectively). However, it is my assertion that, because haikus frequently describe natural features of stunning beauty observed by a single individual (and attempt to do so in the totally non-visual medium of language), the number of syllables one uses when writing a haiku does not really matter. The important thing is that you limit yourself to a short number of set syllables so that you are forced to get to the heart of the thing you are describing, leaving out all superfluous detail and information. Haikus describe something that is, essentially, without meaning (beyond the spiritual impact of having experienced the subject of the haiku), and can only communicate the *resonance* of that experience to the reader. This fact alone makes the exact number of syllables that an individual uses while writing one a total non-issue.

Gutsman: Anyone who remembers the game will recall the endless series of increasingly impossible jumps across the backs of tiny toy helicopters with platforms that would throw you into the abyss at the beginning of this boss' level.

ROBOTNICK: Doctor Robotnick, of Sega's Sonic the Hedgehog games (which were omitted entirely from this book because Sega screwed over their fans by ditching the Dreamcast after having sold more units than any other game system in history) was a bizarre mad scientist who was into two things: floating around in bubbles and creating armies of mechanized animals. The animals he chose were, more often than not, utterly retarded; bloodthirsty bunnies, sea otter sentries, etc.

## A GOOD WALK SPOILED:

"We got your daughter! HA HA HA!" - I swear that this exact quote is used in the intro cinema to one of the games from this genre (most likely Final Fight).

**NOTE:** Double Dragon, Bayou Billy, Final Fight, Streets of Rage, 64th Street, Vigilante (the grandfather of this terrible genre), VC Cops... all of these titles (along with more that I'm sure I've either forgotten or are unfamiliar with) had the same plot and the same gameplay. The madness was unending!

### SMOKING LIGHT GUNS PART II (FROM THE HIP):
I have to say, for the record, that Angee did get very good at House of The Dead.

### DRAGON'S LAIR:
**An interesting note about this game:** During the course of my research for this book, I discovered that the voices for all the characters in the game were done by the staff and animators at Don Bluth's studios to keep the costs down. This really surprised me as the voices were just as memorable as the animation. Another surprising thing: The entire movie of "DRAGON'S LAIR" was only 12 to 22 minutes long (accounts of the length vary)! It just took forever to get through because of dying.

Speaking of which, I did forget to mention how often the bitch with the rolling pin would kill me; for many people I know, this singular hazard would mark the end of their one dollar adventure on this game. That being said, after you figured out what to do, this game was incredible. It was a work of art in every sense; a film that you played, a movie that you participated in. Don Bluth drew you a dream and then invited you in; I still have vivid memories of this game.

### INTERESTING CONCEPT:
Line 3: Streets of Rage (mentioned earlier), a fighting game that I remember mostly due to its emphatic pretense that there was actually a plot to the game. Here's the run down: An attorney's daughter gets kidnapped, so, after getting the ransom phone call, he takes off his suit and (body-builder/Hulk physique thus exposed) takes to the street fighting an endless series of punk hoodlums. Yeah. Ok.

Bayou Billy was another "My girl got kidnapped" game, but, this time, you play the part of a genetically impaired Florida redneck who grins perpetually and enjoys wrestling alligators. This game was not very good but I remember playing the hell out of it along with every other kid I knew.

Line 4: Tempest, literally, the first arcade game I truly enjoyed playing as a kid.

Lines 18-19: Reference to "COMMANDO"

Line 23: A sidescrolling shooter is a game that is designed in 2D using little animated digital pictures called sprites to represent the characters. The emphasis in these games is to traverse a long, horizontal level, killing everything you see. They are also referred to among gaming mags as "Run and Jumpers". Games of this type have been totally replaced by 3D, but, every so often, a new one is put out to keep psychos like me happy.

Line 47: Direct reference to Qix, a Taito game.

Line 69: Centipede, Marble Madness, and 720 (Bees!!!!) (aka SKATE OR DIE!!!!) were all great examples of this.

Lines 55-56: Some examples of being hunted by incontrovertible fates that you are powerless to confront: Hunt the Wumpus, Pac Man, "DEATH" from Gauntlet, Sinistar (the ultimate embodiment of this concept), Contra: The Alien Wars (especially the 2nd level skeleton boss who rips open the side of the building with his multiple robotic alien heads; there, you couldn't even run!), SHODAN from System Shock, every fighting game ever made, Bioforge (a great Origin title for PC), ONE for the original Playstation, Missile Command, Defender, ROBOTRON ("DOT DOT HUMANOID!!!"), Lode Runner, etc. etc. etc.

Line 96: "a moving formalism..." The game that really embodies this in my mind is Tempest 2000 for the defunct Jaguar... it really was a beautiful thing to play, colors dancing and exploding around the simple geometric lines that formed the playfield. I miss this game. I miss this system.

Line 82: Mary K's, Big Dipper, Red Rock Cinema, Charleston Heights Bowling, (which later became Arizona Charlie's), Caeser's Palace Arcade (I liked that one a lot), The Paddle Wheel Arcade... all gone now, all gone...

Line 89: Jungle Hunt springs to mind.

## A VERY SPECIAL MESSAGE FROM MAJOR HAVOC:

**Fan Boy Moment:** The "intro cinema" (this game was vector drawn) had the greatest line in it about the clones: "You are them, they are you. All from one, one from all." Man, Owen R. Rubin and the rest of them fat cats at Atari were cool! **END OF FAN BOY MOMENT.**

## ASTROSMASH:

**General Note:** The Blue Sky Rangers were the guys behind Intellivision. They are still around today and own the rights to all their old games. You can buy PC versions of nearly all your favorites at www.intellivisionlives.com, but what's really cool is that they are releasing game pads that you plug into your TV that have the games BUILT IN! Oh, the joy; Astrosmash and Thunder Castle back on my TV! (Thunder Castle, incidentally, has been unavailable in any format other than the original Intellivision console; no ROMs were converted or ripped for PC, so this will be the first time that The Unfinished Symphony (Intellivision arrangement) will be heard by my ears in eighteen years!)

## MISSILE COMMAND:

Dave Theurer, the programmer of Missile Command, really did have nightmares while writing the game (and, from what I've read on the web, for six months after it was completed).

## BUBBLE BOBBLE:

The silliest poem in this book by far, I could not bring myself to cut it simply because the game that it's about is just as silly as the poem itself.

## PAC MAN:

This game really did fill me with an uneasy sense of dread and impending doom rather than imparting feelings of fun and excitement. To put it plainly, let me just explain the facts behind the basic premise of this, one of the most well known games ever: You are trapped in a maze from which there is no escape. There are five ghosts that you are unable to kill (unless you collect a power pellet). The ghosts' sole intent, their entire reason for existence, is to kill you. Even if you do manage to kill them, they come back to life a short time later and resume hunting you. Now you tell me if that doesn't sound like a nightmare.

## DEFENDER:

Still, to this day, I have no idea how to play this game properly.

## BOSS ENCOUNTERS:

The "game" in this poem does not exist. Rather, it is a composite of many memories I have from playing a lot of similar games from the space shooter genre. R-TYPE (& II), Lifeforce (really gross), Gradius, Darius (they said: "let there be fish and fire" and there was, and it was fun), were all used in this poem.

## COCKTAIL MODE:

During my hunt for Major Havoc (I spent over a hundred and

fifty hours searching for the name of this game and looked through every entry in the KLOV up to the M's), I came across a webpage that had a transcript from an article in "Time" Magazine. The article claimed that video games had become so popular that businessmen could be found swarming around arcades during lunch hour. I don't know if the trend could possibly have been as extreme as the article made it sound, but I find it comforting to think that it was.

### COUNTER-STRIKE (Or: Black Elvis):

This poem is true. He's still out there, somewhere, waiting for the "GO!" command. If you happen to run into him, tell him that Skookie says "hi!", and that I really am a writer and that I really did write a poem about him; hope all is well, big guy.

### SKOOKIE SPRITE:

Skookie was my nickname in Counter-Strike (one of the greatest multiplayer PC games of all time). You can find my CLQ player ID on my web page at: www.twhi.org/twhicspages.htm

The best I ever ranked on the CLQ was in the top 3,000 players (I only hung in there for a few weeks). For those who have not visited The Champion's League Quake (The CLQ), they keep track of ten million players' stats and then rank all of them based on kills versus deaths and how quickly they kill. If 3,000 sounds pretty good to you, well, it was, but I knew people who had been ranked in the top 20!

### LIVING ROOM BALLET:

This poem is about Virtua Fighter 4 (for the PS2).

### KAGE:

This poem is also true; there really were (and, as far as I know, still are) ninjas living in my parent's garage.
Also: I've read on the KLOV that "kage" is Japanese for "shadow," and, because this is a golden opportunity to finally answer a great lurking mystery from my childhood, I should also mention that it's pronounced Kah-geh ("geh" as in "get," but without the "t") not "cage".

### THE LONG NIGHT OF THE LAW:

I never got as far as this poem depicts in the vigilante missions in GTA:VC. The highest level I've been to is 232, at which point, I quit.

# Appendix E:
# Resources and Suggested Reading

http://www.csd.uwo.ca/Infocom/zork1.html - Remember ZORK? Want to download it, play it, and sing its praises without the hindrance of monetary transaction? Then check out this page, download the game, and resume the grue hunting you abandoned twenty years ago!

www.KLOV.com - The Killer List of Video Games, one of the most stunningly comprehensive resources for video game related information I've ever seen. They have hundreds of thousands of arcade machines catalogued on this site and are linked to information in The International Video Game Museum.

www.donbluth.com - Don Bluth Studios, the folks behind "Dragon's Lair" and "The Secret of NIMH" ("It's moving day!"). This is a great site dedicated to preserving the art of hand-drawn film animation, but what's really cool is the store. They have original art cells from the game, really awesome Dragon's Lair posters (autographed by Don Bluth and Gary Goldman!), and a whole host of other incredibly cool stuff.

http://members.tripod.com/~PitfallHarry/ - Pitfall Harry's Lost Video Game Cavern is one of those rare and totally psychotic fan sites that is at once disturbing in its sincerity while simultaneously managing to charm its visitors. Worth checking out for whimsy's sake.

www.inform-fiction.org/ - Contains the Inform compiler, a well-documented programming utility that greatly simplifies the process of creating your own text based adventure games.

www.classicgaming.com - One of the best sites on all that is old and 8-bit, Classic Gaming is a great site for those wishing to return to the glory days of their favorite games (be they arcade machines, consoles, etc.). This site is a must.

www.mobygames.com - A great attempt at creating a comprehensive index of all video gamedom past and present, the content on this site comes from its users (administrators fact-check every entry, though, to ensure accuracy). Check it out and contribute some of your favorite titles if they're not listed.

www.twingalaxies.com - Twin Galaxies Internet Scoreboard. Remember the old days of gaming when everyone was scrabbling for the high score on a popular machine? Well, apparently, those days never ended. This site keeps a running tab on the current high scores for arcade and console games and has recently published a book of world records of video games.

http://www.planetstarsiege.com/allyourbase/ - For Great Justice! All Your Base Are Belong To Us. Zig Thanks You.

www.1up-zine.com - The homepage for 1-up Mega Zine, one of the coolest zines on the subject that is being produced today.

www.thegamingproject.com - Another historic first in the world of video gaming, The Gaming Project is the homepage for "Gamers: A Documentary," a new DVD that focuses on the interpersonal relationships spawned by Counter-Strike.

www.twhi.org/bluewizard.htm - The homepage for this book with links to more old games pages, poems that were omitted from this book (Voldo, Rastan, and several others), ordering information, links to other books published by Rusty Immelman Press, and all manner of useless divertments. Bonus Levels: User: greenelf Pass: konami (of course!)

# ALL YOUR BASE
# ARE BELONG
# TO US!

What book of poems about video games could possibly be complete without mentioning (in some way) this, the most glorious artistic achievement to be inspired by a video game? The "lyrics" for *All Your Base* (a killer meme put out by some punk hoodlum kids at Stanford) come from an old Taoplan Genesis game called "Zero Wing" (which was a port of the arcade machine of the same name). The following dialogue is delivered via jerky cut scenes of a spaceship in peril at the beginning of the game. "Cats" is the evil bad guy who has "set up us the bomb." Remember: Zig thanks you.


Zero Wing Intro Script:
IN A.D. 2101
WAR WAS BEGINNING.
CAPTAIN : WHAT HAPPEN ?
MECHANIC : SOMEBODY SET UP US THE BOMB.
OPERATOR : WE GET SIGNAL.
CAPTAIN : WHAT !
OPERATOR : MAIN SCREEN TURN ON.
CAPTAIN : IT'S YOU !
CATS : HOW ARE YOU GENTLEMEN !!
CATS : ALL YOUR BASE ARE BELONG TO US.
CATS : YOU ARE ON THE WAY TO DESTRUCTION.
CAPTAIN : WHAT YOU SAY !!
CATS : YOU HAVE NO CHANCE TO SURVIVE
         MAKE YOUR TIME.
CATS : HA HA HA HA ....
OPERATOR : CAPTAIN !!
CAPTAIN : TAKE OFF EVERY 'ZIG'!!
CAPTAIN : YOU KNOW WHAT YOU DOING.
CAPTAIN : MOVE 'ZIG'
CAPTAIN : FOR GREAT JUSTICE.
TITLE SCREEN

## Credits:
### (Cue the bad 80's synth-based fusion jazz)

The Programming Team of Rusty Immelman Press wishes to express our most sincere gratitude to the following people and organizations for their cooperation and assistance during the creation of this book:

The Killer List of Video Games (www.klov.com)
Classic Gaming.com
Mameworld.net
Warren Wucinich for his creative input and dogged adherence to
        deadlines
John Pham of Epoxy Press and Raina Lee of 1-Up Mega Zine
Angee Jackson (artistic genius and "queen of the scene")
Vessy Ivanova, creative consultation
Jessie Smigel
Jorpho of ClassicGaming.com for help with fact checking
Tim Arnold, future curator of the international pinball museum
        (we hope!)
Don Bluth Studios for graciously allowing us to reproduce and
        use the image of Dirk the Daring
Demian Linn and Dan "Shoe" Hsu, for taking the time to grant
        us their opinion on the project
Darren and Holli of Brewske's and the entire Brewske's team for
        housing editorial meetings (and other drinking binges).
Jarret Keene and Meredith McGhan for supporting the project
The many thousands of programmers who, through their Promethian
        efforts, have made it possible to play most of the games
        mentioned in this book by using MAME
Fresh Printz of Las Vegas
Sarah Frank of Phoenix Color Corporation
and last, but certainly not least: Owen R. Rubin & Jed Margolin
        for being the programming masters that they are

If you used cheat codes to get this far in the book, you will have to go back to the beginning and read it again at a harder difficulty level.

### Continue?
10 9 8 7 6 5 4 3 2 1 0
### GAME OVER
Thank You For Playing!

About The Author:

Seth "Fingers" Flynn Barkan is a poet, composer, Stride Pianist, music tutor, freelance writer, video game enthusiast, and lunatic at large. Some of his other works include: "Your Madness and You (An Instructional Pamphlet)", and "A Cacophony of Near-Fatal Mistakes" (published by Jazzclaw, an imprint of Searle Publishing, UK). He is the madman behind the "Skookie Script Suite," a set of scripts written to make playing Counter-Strike easier and more fun, and is the author of the Grand Theft Auto: Vice City Vigilante Missions FAQ. He lives in an immense gothic castle filled with video games and pinball machines somewhere on the outskirts of Fabulous Las Vegas. He is 23, and, despite his busy music and writing careers, still manages to find time to play video games on a daily basis. He is currently working on his next book.

About the Illustrator:

Warren Wucinich joined the Rusty Immelman Press Team during a drinking contest held at Cheers Bar and Grill and has stuck with us ever since. A devestatingly talented individual, he is currently at work on a slew of graphic novel collaborations and other artistic projects. He can be found working as a caricaturist on the Las Vegas Strip and is currently training to become a professional assassin.

# Other Titles From Rusty Immelman Press

If you, or someone you love, is deeply and horrifically psychotic, you will love some of these other books published by R.i.P:

### They Call Me Mojo: The Poetry of Conrad Lochner
One of the most ragged and intelligent voices to break out on the poetry scene in years, Lochner stuns and amazes his readers with vivid accounts of DMV lines, nature walks on shrooms, and much more.

### A Cacophony of Near-Fatal Mistakes (Spoken Word CD)
Seth "Fingers" Flynn Barkan reads 20 of his poems (most taken from the collection of the same name) set to original music. Includes: "Losing At Pool," "News of the World, Mother; News of the World," and other, best-loved favorites. Music ranges in style from Big Band and Stride to "Music From The Hearts of Space"-type synth. 72 mins. playtime.

### Your Madness And You: An Instructional Pamphlet
Doktor Nicodemus Strangelove reunites with his wily and demented cohort Ideline VonHozzlenugen once again, this time to save the world from the horrible "pneumonic madness plague," a malady that twists otherwise normal individuals into hopelessly depressed psychotic introverts. Save your sanity: Read this chapbook before it's too late!

## Coming Soon:

### An Account of the Virginia City Camel Races
Conrad Lochner kidnaps his hapless readers and drags them on a drug induced psychotic trip-out to the camel, emu, and ostrich races held annually in Northern Nevada.

### The Poetry of Meredith McGhan (Working Title)
A ridiculously credited and widely-published poet, McGhan is the most scholarly addition to the Rusty Immelman Press family of reprobates and lunatics. Representing everything that can go right in academic poetry, her work is sure to thrill and delight any true poetry enthusiast. Look for this title during National Poetry Month.

## Coming Soon (Cont.)

### THESE IS THE POEMS! Celebrating 14 Decades of Rusty Immelman Press' Literary Journal In the Las Vegas Valley

Various voices of the damned denizens of Las Vegas (past and present) collected, arranged, and orchestrated into one chorus of semi-satirical pain. Release Date TBA.

### Drunk On The Moon: Poetry From the Bars of Vegas

Little is known about this strange and mysterious title. Working from a manuscript we found in the men's room of a dive bar, we are currently researching the identity of the poet behind this book in order to secure the rights to its publication.

**For more information** on these (or any other) titles published by Rusty Immelman Press, please visit us on the web at: *www.twhi.org/immelman.htm* Once there, you can browse our online catalogue, read samples of current and upcoming releases, hear musical and spoken word clips of our authors reading, see photos, play games (all sorts), and enjoy other useless divertments all without the hinderance of monetary transaction. You can also join our mailing list (we do not share your information with anyone, ever) and receive emails (ONLY) when our authors are reading in your area.

**Also** be sure to visit our snack bar in Charleston Grotto (all sales are final, void where prohibited by law).

**IF YOU ARE INTERESTED** in submitting your material to Rusty Immelman Press, please do not send any manuscripts before reading our submission guidelines, which can be found on our website.

### If you liked this book... Help Fight Writer Attrition: *Send Fan Mail!*

We pay our writers mere pennies; make someone's day with words of praise! Address correspondence to: *immelman@twhi.org*

**Rusty Immelman Press**
4075 S. Durango Dr., Suite #111-72
Las Vegas, NV 89147-4158

**To Order More Copies of Blue Wizard Is About To Die!**, please fill out the following form and send with check or money order to the address on the opposite side. Please make checks payable to Rusty Immelman Press.

Name:_____

Address:_____

_____

_____

Email:_____

Phone:_____

Qty (NOTE: Free shipping on orders of 2 or more!):_____

Shipping (for single-copy orders): $5

Subtotal: Qty. x $15 =_____

Signed? (makes a great gift!) + $10 per copy =_____

      Note: Please be sure to include a note clearly listing the names

      of the people to whom the book should be signed.

      + shipping =_____

Total:_____

Thank you for your order! Please allow 3-4 weeks for delivery.
If you have any questions, please do not hesitate to contact us via email at orders@twhi.org.

Rusty Immelman Press is committed to ensuring your satisfaction. If you are dissatisfied with your purchase (for any reason), simply return your book for a full refund (minus shipping costs). You can cancel this order at any time.

You can pay by credit card by ordering our books through our website at: www.twhi.org/bluewizard.htm